ACKNOWLEDGEMENTS

I would like to thank all those kind people who helped me gather the material for this book: Ken Barrett, Felix Bieger, Phillip Bruce, Nick Demuth, Marvin Farkas, David Mahoney, Ian Markham-Smith, Nicola Parkinson, Jonathan Wattis and many others. Particular thanks are due to David Roads—the man who first broke the story of the 'Human Yo-Yo'—who provided me with copious notes on General Aguinaldo and Dr Rizal. Thanks are also due to Penelope Byrne and the Hong Kong Tourist Association, Cliff Dunnaway of the Hong Kong Historical Aircraft Association and the staff of the Public Records Office. My special thanks go to South China Morning Post, where some of this material has already been published, and Judy Young and the staff of the South China Morning Post Library.

THE
HONG KONG
VISITORS BOOK

A HISTORICAL WHO'S WHO

THE HONG KONG VISITORS BOOK

A HISTORICAL WHO'S WHO

by

Arthur Hacker

ODYSSEY

An Odyssey Publication © 1997
Text © Arthur Hacker 1997

Published by The Guidebook Company Limited, Hong Kong

Photo & illustrations credits:

Most of the illustrations in this book are a part of the Arthur Hacker Collection of old photographs, prints and postcards of Hong Kong, Macau, China and Japan. The reproduction rights of this collection are managed by the Stock House Photoagency, 23rd Floor, 88 Lockhart Road, Wanchai, Hong Kong. Tel: 2866-0887 • Fax: 2866-2212.

Grateful acknowledgment is made to the following:

Airphoto International Ltd: 19, 194-5; Archives & Manuscripts University Libraries. Arizona State University (Temple): 187; Department of Kuomintang Party History: 184, 185; Marvin Farkas: 162-3; Government Information Services: 20-1, 179, 191; Hongkong & Shanghai Bank: 16-17, 55; Hong Kong Historical Aircraft Society: 151-3; Hong Kong Museum of Art: 40, 42-3; Hong Kong Museum of History: 104-5, 133, 204; Hongkong Standard Newspapers Ltd: 211; Hong Kong Tourist Association 85, 213; Hong Kong University Library: 25; Hulton Deutsch Collection Ltd: 123, 163, 167, 178, 197, 198, 182, 207, 229; Luk Kwok Hotel: 204; National Archives of Canada: 212; National Portrait Gallery: 79; John Oliver: 192, 223; The Peninsula: 168, 201; Rizal Museum, Manila: 135; Smithsonian Institution, National Portrait Gallery: 98; South China Morning Post Library: 193; Times of India: 223; US Army Military History Institute: 153; Virago Press: 101; Yau Leung: 202-3; (Copyright applied for: 204).

The generous support of the Hong Kong Tourist Association is greatly appreciated by the publishers.

Project Managing Editor: Rebecca Ridolfo
Editors: Cherry Barnett and Steven Lloyd
Illustrations Editor: John Oliver
Designer: Teresa Ho Kit Mei • Training Design Graphics
Cover Design: Harvey Symons

Odyssey Publications / The Guidebook Company Limited, Hong Kong
Ground Floor, 14 Lower Kai Yuen Lane, North Point, Hong Kong.
Tel: (852) 2856 3896 Fax: (852) 2565 8624

Printed in Hong Kong

ISBN: 962-217-417-5
British Library Cataloguing in Publication Data has been applied for.

CONTENTS

INTRODUCTION

This book is about people who have visited Hong Kong; who they were, what they did and what they thought about the place. First impressions are often very vivid, even though they are sometimes bizarre, bigoted and bewilderingly inaccurate. When I arrived in Hong Kong in 1967, I expected to find a golden city of domes and pagodas, in the heart of a primæval forest, inhabited by exotic Chinese girls with cheongsams slit up to their armpits. I was in for a shock.

It was December, bitterly cold in the concrete jungle and Maoist bombs were going off all over the place. I turned on the television set and there was my next door neighbour from Aldershot (the 'home' of the British Army) reading the news on Rediffusion. Somewhat despondent I went down to the hotel coffee shop for a sandwich and, when it came, the crust had been cut off the bread. This was something that I hadn't seen in England since before World War Two. The coffee shop was called 'Camelot' and the Chinese waiters were dressed like mediæval pages in baggy red and yellow tights. The sartorial logic was that the hotel was called the 'Merlin'. It is now defunct. 'Mort d'Arthur', I thought...After that things got better; they could hardly have got worse.

Hong Kong seemed so unreal that after a couple of weeks I was firmly convinced that it only existed in my imagination. Nowadays I find London, Paris and New York a trifle odd. If you live in any place long enough, the strange ceases to be strange and the unusual becomes the norm. This is why visitors' impressions of a city are often more interesting than those of a longtime resident.

A description of a place is also very much determined by the character of the writer. Puritans like the Reverend John Arthur Turner found sin wherever he looked; but he was the sort of cleric who would be quite capable of finding debauchery in the Kingdom of Heaven, if he ever got that far. If an old soldier like James Bodell, who had spent half his life knocking around the grogshops and goldfields of Australia, found Hong Kong a bit rough, then you can be certain that it *was* a bit rough. All reports are biased to a greater or lesser extent.

This is a record of what a number of individuals, from a couple of dozen different countries with vastly different backgrounds and conflicting opinions, thought about Hong Kong. Sir Miles Lampson found

Chinese food 'positively nasty'. While it may be considered 'politically incorrect' to mention this, I have included it simply because that is what he wrote in his private diary. The food was probably superb, but Sir Miles didn't like it and said so.

A conscientious historian will check and double check with two or three reliable sources before committing a word to paper. I have recorded what people wrote at the time. It was not always the truth. Trebitsch Lincoln and Captain 'Bully' Hayes are not truly reliable sources. They were both compulsive liars.

When quoting from books and particularly from old Hong Kong newspapers, which are also not famous for their accuracy, I have not always identified the origin of every single quotation. This is because I did not want the stories to become cluttered with masses of references and annotations. It does not matter too much to the general reader if an article appeared in the *China Mail* or the *Hongkong Telegraph*. A bibliography is included at the back of the book for the curious.

What I have attempted to do is reflect the ambiance and atmosphere of Hong Kong as seen through the eyes of its visitors, many of whom are famous, but also through others who are almost unknown.

History repeats itself; and historians repeat each other, as well as themselves. Some of what I have written has appeared before in my other books or in my articles in the *South China Morning Post* and the *Hong Kong Tatler*. 'History is the distillation of rumour,' wrote Scotland's greatest historian, Thomas Carlyle. This book contains a modest amount of rumour.

Travel used to be a great experience; it still can be, but it has become much easier today, particularly if you are rich or famous. You cannot pick up a Hong Kong newspaper without reading that yet another celebrity is in town. Some of them do not even leave their hotel rooms, except to attend a press conference to promote their latest film, themselves or some equally worthy cause. With a couple of exceptions, I have not written about this sort of visitor. Nowadays, almost everybody who is anybody drops into Hong Kong at sometime. It has been claimed that if you lingered around the Star Ferry for long enough you would eventually meet everybody you know—or might like to know.

HONG KONG: A HISTORICAL VIEW

*H*ong Kong has a short but complicated history, which is interlinked irrevocably with that of China. In order to enjoy this book, it is useful to know something of the events leading up to Hong Kong becoming a British Crown Colony and a little of the history of the colonial years.

At the beginning of the last century, China had been ruled for more than 250 years by the Manchus—or Tartars, as they were sometimes called. They were a warlike nation from the north-east. Although Manchuria is now part of China, traditionally it was regarded by the Han Chinese as a foreign country and the Ching dynasty of the Manchus— or *Qing* as it is now spelled*—was considered a foreign power. Dr Sun Yat- sen was always complaining about 'the cruelty of the Tartar yoke'.

The Manchus were not the only 'foreigners' to rule in China. The
Mongols held power for over a century during the Yuan Dynasty, but
China has always had the capacity to 'sinicise' its conquerors.

The Chinese called their country the Middle Kingdom and all
foreigners were either barbarians or, in the case of the British and
Americans, outer barbarians. The forlorn attempts of these outer
barbarians to establish diplomatic relations with China were regarded
by the Imperial Court as ridiculous. They were vassal states—and that
was that. Unlike Siam (Thailand) and Japan, there was rarely a credible
attempt by the Manchu rulers to find out anything about the West.

All foreign trade, restricted to the southern port of Canton, was

*Panoramic view of Hong
Kong in 1886*

between a group of Chinese traders called the Co Hong Guild of Merchants and the great East India Companies of the West. This arrangement suited both China and the East India Companies. The Westerners paid for tea, silk and porcelain with silver, which was all the Chinese would accept and which was cheap in the West at the time. Early in the last century a number of events, caused mainly by the Napoleonic Wars, upset this cosy arrangement. The massive East India Companies either collapsed under their own weight and went bankrupt, or their monopolies were taken away by their own governments.

When the Honourable East India Company explained to the Ching mandarins that they had lost their monopoly, the British government was asked to send out a new head man to take charge of the British merchants in Canton. They sent Lord Napier. The Manchus had expected them to send a trader, but Napier was a diplomat. From the Ching point of view, to accept his credentials was tantamount to acknowledging that the British monarch was the equal of the Emperor of China. This was treason. They gave poor old Napier the nickname 'Laboriously Vile' and hounded him out of Canton in 1834. He died a broken man in Macau. This did not go down very well in Westminster.

Even before the demise of the East India Companies, a new breed of trader had appeared on the China coast. These were known as the 'interlopers': hard men like William Jardine, James Matheson and Lancelot Dent. The import of opium had been banned in China and the Honourable East India Company's ships did not carry the drug. The interlopers, however, had no such scruples. There was smuggling on a massive scale. Often their partners in crime were corrupt mandarins who allowed, for a large bribe, the war junks of the Opium Suppression Force to be hired for smuggling purposes. Opium had even replaced silver as the main currency of China's international trade. As well as ruining the health of millions of Chinese, it was destroying the economy and silver was flowing out of the country at an alarming rate.

The situation got so completely out of hand that, in 1838, the Ching

14

Emperor sent Commissioner Lin Tse-hsu to Canton to sort out the matter. Both Lin and the British Plenipotentiary, Captain Charles Elliot, were honourable well-meaning men, but they found it impossible to communicate with each other. The difference between the two cultures was simply too great. From both points of view it was like trying to conduct negotiations with creatures from outer space. War became inevitable. Opium may have been the spark, but it was only one of the causes of the conflagration which followed.

It was an unequal struggle. The clumsy war junks had no chance against the awesome firepower and manoeuvrability of the British war steamers. Manchu bannermen, who for some reason favoured bows and arrows even though they had firearms, discovered that the percussion muskets of the British regiments were far more effective.

When the Union Jack was raised over Hong Kong in 1841, there were only about 5,000 Chinese living on the island and they were mainly fishermen and pirates. By the middle of the 1850s the total population had risen to over 70,000; of which a paltry 500 were British. This did not include their protectors, the British garrison, which stood at about 5,000. Sadly, Hong Kong had not become the great emporium of trade envisaged by its founders. Instead, Shanghai

Sidney Hall's map of Hong Kong, published in 1818

Hong Kong at the turn of the century

was the centre of the China trade. This city was one of the five treaty
ports opened up to the West as a result of the Treaty of Nanking, finally
ratified in 1843, which had ceded Hong Kong Island to Great Britain in
perpetuity.

Succeeding British governments instructed the governors of Hong
Kong to avoid armed conflict with China, if possible. In 1856 the fifth
Governor of Hong Kong, Sir John Bowring, started a war over a trivial
incident involving a Chinese lorcha called the *Arrow*. When parliament
heard about the war (three months after it had started) they voted out
the Whig government and there was a general election. But the Whigs
were re-elected and the war continued intermittently until 1860.

Aided by the French, the British captured Peking and forced the
Emperor to allow them the right to set up legations in the capital. More
treaty ports were opened to the West; Hong Kong's prize was the
Kowloon peninsula. Meanwhile, refugees from the Taiping Rebellion in
China (1851–64) poured into Hong Kong in their thousands. By the end

of the century, other European nations were establishing foreign concessions in many parts of China. In 1898 the New Territories were leased by Britain for ninety-nine years.

The Boxer Rebellion, which came to a head in 1900, heralded the death knell of Imperial China, although the Ching dynasty did not fall until 1911. On New Year's Day 1912, Dr Sun Yat-sen became the first President of the Chinese Republic. China was at last ruled again by the Han Chinese. Six weeks later he resigned. For the next twenty years the warlords fought each other and China was in turmoil. In 1931, after Chiang Kai-shek's Nationalists had gained the upper hand, Japan invaded Manchuria. More refugees flooded into the colony. The total population was well over a million when Japan captured Hong Kong on Christmas Day 1941.

Hong Kong was liberated in 1945 and civil war broke out again in China in the following year. The People's Republic of China was established in 1949 under the leadership of Mao Tse-tung, an event which was followed by another vast influx of refugees into Hong Kong. This time they came to stay. Whole factories, including machines and workers, were shipped in from Shanghai. As a result, in a generation Hong Kong was transformed from a sleepy colonial entrepôt on the south China coast into the mighty industrial society it is today. It now has a population of over six million.

The lease on the New Territories runs out in 1997; then Hong Kong will become a Special Administrative Region within China. The most frequent question asked today is: what will happen after 1997? The only sensible reply seems to be: wait and see.

> * *Pinyin* is now the official system for the romanization of the Chinese script: Ching becomes *Qing*, Peking becomes *Beijing* and Mao Tse-tung becomes *Mao Zedong* but, by convention, the spelling of Sun Yat-sen and Chiang Kai-shek remain unchanged. All very confusing for the general reader. For reasons related to quotations—where it would be incorrect to make alterations—I have decided to leave all Chinese names in their traditional spelling.

(following pages)
Auguste Borget's lithograph of a village square in Hong Kong before it became a British colony

17

HAN YU
CHINESE POET

A thousand years before the British arrived in Hong Kong, Han Yu, the legendary Tang Dynasty poet, visited Castle Peak and 'ascended the mountain of Tuen Mun and looked over the vast unfathomable ocean and the forests and the waters and felt that it was indeed a sacred spot'. There is a four-character inscription carved on a massive granite boulder at Castle Peak, which is attributed to the poet. It translates roughly as 'The Finest High Mountain'. Today, standing on Han Yu's 'sacred spot' looking west, you can see the elegant chimneys of Castle Peak Power Station and, looking south, you have a glorious panoramic view of Tuen Mun New Town.

In one of his poems, describing a storm at sea, he wrote:

> 'They say that Tuen Mun is a high mountain,
> But even these waves will swallow it up.'

Today, it is the pollution—not the waves—that threaten to engulf the 'Sacred Mountain'.

Han Yu was well connected. His grand-nephew was Han Hsiang Tzu, one of the Eight Immortals of Chinese mythology. The Han family seem to have spent most of their time arguing with each other in verse. Han Yu was also a Taoist. He got into trouble when he criticised the Emperor for having a relic of Buddha in his palace. The Emperor exiled him to Chao Chou in Guangdong province. The Pearl River Delta at that time was infested with crocodiles. Han Yu was asked to get rid of them. Being a poet, he composed a poem entitled 'Address to the Crocodiles' and threw it in the river.

It began:

> 'The great ocean spreads in the South.
> There live huge whales and monster birds,
> Tiny shrimps and little crabs:
> All creatures find space and nourishment therein.
>
> If the crocodiles start in the morning
> They will reach the sea by nightfall.'

We are told that the Chinese water crocodiles, an endangered species even in the time of the Tang Dynasty, followed his absurd advice and, as a consequence, the reptile is now extinct.

20

The New Territories, with the New Town of Tuen Mun below Castle Peak

Han Yu's grand-nephew, Han Hsiang Tzu

HUANG KU
SUNG DYNASTY PRINCESS

*G*enghis Khan's invasion of China in 1211 was not the first time Mongols had attacked the 'Celestial Empire'. Almost a hundred years earlier the Mongol hordes had swept through the Middle Kingdom with relentless fury. In 1127 they even managed to capture the Sung Emperor Kao Tsung and all his family—except his ten-year-old daughter who escaped.

The ladies of the court took the royal child and fled south. After many adventures they ran into a band of loyalist militia commanded by a member of the Tang family. He hid the little princess in Kam Tin in the New Territories, where his clan was very powerful. They even owned Hong Kong Island at the time.

The story goes that the little princess fell passionately in love with her rescuer's son, Tang Tzu-ming, and that they were married. Meanwhile, her father had established a truce with the Mongols and began to wonder what had happened to his daughter. He sent messengers far and wide to find her.

*Statue of the
Military God of Wealth, Kam Tin*

Statue of Kam Kang

22

This put the fear of God into the Tangs, as the marriage had taken place without the Emperor's consent. However, the noble princess returned to court with her terrified husband. The loving couple were forgiven. The princess soon decided that she disliked the sophisticated court life and returned to tranquil Kam Tin, where she was known locally as 'Huang Ku', which means 'Emperor's Aunt'.

In the twilight of her incredibly virtuous life, the princess was faced with the unpleasant task of selecting a grave site for herself. She eventually decided on Lion Hill near Shek Lung. Her *fung shui* advisor told her that, if she was buried at the head of the lion, her descendants would be great men. However, if she was buried at the tail, they were destined forever to be humble folk and eat red rice and herrings. Predictably, she chose the tail. The fortunes of the Tang clan have gone downhill ever since.

Statue of the Civil God of Wealth

Statue of an earth god

WEI WONG
LAST SUNG EMPEROR

———◆———

In 1277 the Mongol hordes of Kublai Khan swept through southern China. Yi Wong, the boy Emperor, fled to Lantau Island and set up court at Mui Wo (Silvermine Bay), where he died the next year. He was succeeded by his brother, seven-year-old Wei Wong, who was the last Emperor of the Sung Dynasty.

The Sung Emperor's Terrace, Kowloon

Wei Wong and his court moved from Lantau to the mainland. Legend has it that one day the boy Emperor stood overlooking Lei Yue Mun. 'I have counted eight mountains,' said the child, 'so there must be eight dragons hereabout.'

'In reality there are nine dragons in this locality, Your Majesty,' replied his favourite courtier, while grovelling at his feet.

'There are only eight dragons!' squealed the indignant child. 'I have counted them!'

'Your Majesty's sacred person is the ninth dragon,' explained the courtier. Kowloon means 'nine dragons' in Chinese and that, according to legend, is how Kowloon got its name.

The Emperor lived for a time in a cave under a giant rock in Kowloon. This great boulder was known as the Sung Emperor's Terrace. When the British acquired the New Territories in 1898, under the terms of the lease they were required to preserve this sacred site. The Hong Kong Government built a splendid granite balustrade around the

24

boulder and it became a holy place for pilgrims. During World War Two the rock was broken up by the Japanese and the stones were used to enlarge Kai Tak Airport.

Poor little Wei Wong's army was no match for the Mongols. After a series of defeats he was cornered by Kublai Khan's fleet and his forces were destroyed in a ferocious sea battle in the Pearl River Delta. The boy Emperor drowned trying to escape. For the next century China was ruled by the Mongols. This period is known as the Yuan Dynasty.

Mongol Warships

SIMAO D'ANDRADE
ADVENTURER

*T*he British were not the first Western nation to found a colony in Hong Kong. The Portuguese sailor Jorge Alvares first arrived at Tuen Mun in the New Territories in 1514. At the time it was an important anchorage for foreign merchants—mainly Arabs, Indians and Persians.

Four years later, as a result of Alvares' voyage, the Portuguese sent Fernando d'Andrāde to open trade negotiations with the Chinese authorities in Canton. He had limited success. The next year he was replaced by his brother, Simao d'Andrāde.

Fernando had shown tact, diplomacy and, above all, patience; all of which are considered necessary virtues when negotiating with the Chinese. Simao was exactly the opposite: arrogant, hot-headed and impetuous.

The talks floundered after Simao clobbered a Chinese official. He built a fort, put up boundary markers and raised the Portuguese flag in an attempt to found a trading colony. Historians are vague as to the exact location of the place. Opinions vary from Tsuen Wan, Kwai Chung or Tuen Mun itself.

From his fortress, Simao launched a campaign against the pirates who infested the Pearl River Delta. He ended up by becoming a pirate himself—attacking ships, burning villages and generally terrorising the area.

Retribution was swift. The Mandarin Wang Hung attacked and destroyed most of the Portuguese ships with fire-boats. Among those killed was Jorge Alvares, who was probably the first European to land in Hong Kong. Wang Hung then besieged the fort for three months. One dark September night in 1521, during a violent thunderstorm, three Portuguese ships managed to slip their cables, evade the Chinese fleet and escape, just before the fortress was destroyed and its defenders put to the sword. A Portuguese fleet arrived the next year, only to be defeated by the indomitable war junks of Wang Hung in a ferocious battle off San Wui. It was some thirty years before the caravels of the King of Portugal were seen again on the Pearl River.

Detail of an old Chinese map showing Tuen Mun.
Hong Kong Island is identified with the Chinese characters for 'Red Incense Burner'.

A Tartar of the Chinese Army.

The Tiger

A Tartar Soldier, a Tiger Guard and an Archer, by William Alexander

Chinese junks, by William Alexander

AUGUSTE BORGET
FRENCH ARTIST

'I am at last in China. I have taken possession of the Celestial Empire,' wrote the French artist Auguste Borget in 1838. Three years later Sir Edward Belcher said more or less the same thing when he raised the Union Jack at Possession Point, Hong Kong.

Borget was one of the few Europeans to visit Hong Kong before it became a British colony. He also did some beautiful drawings of it. Three of his studies of Hong Kong appear as lithographs in his book *La Chine et Les Chinois*. They were copied rather badly by the English artist, Thomas Allom. Unfortunately, his copies are better known today than Borget's originals. Allom, unlike Borget, never set foot in China.

Borget lived aboard the French frigate *Psyche* and would go ashore every day to sketch. The Hong Kong fisherfolk were poor, yet quite hospitable. They asked him into their houses and gave him tea and fish and rice. Borget was not very good with chopsticks. This was because his technique was basically flawed. He described how he held a 'little stick' in each hand, watched solemnly by the fishermen's children, who munched away at his ham sandwiches. Eventually he was given a spoon.

He arrived in Canton in the middle of the opium crisis. The European population was confined to a space of a few hundred square feet on the waterfront, called the 'Factories.' Officially, they were not allowed into the city of Canton or the surrounding countryside. However, the waterways were neutral and Borget and his friends would take out a boat for the day. Consequently, most of his pictures are of river scenes. When things began to get unpleasant in Canton, Borget retreated to Macau.

A few months later a Manchu army threatened the enclave. Borget visited their camp and was so impressed by the archery of the troops that he did a drawing. However, bows and arrows proved to be no match for 'Paddy' Gough's artillery. Borget, had wisely left Macau by the time the Opium War started in 1839.

(Preceding pages)
*A Bamboo Aquaduct
in Hong Kong,
by Auguste Borget*

*A village near Canton,
by Auguste Borget*

*A salt merchant's house
on the Honan Canal,
Canton*

A wood-engraving of Borget's drawing of cooked food stalls in Canton

38

Borget's lithograph of a triumphal arch between Macau and Canton

*A merchant unloading goods
at a Canton factory*

A group of beggars, Canton

An itinerant cleaner of ears

EDWARD CREE
NAVAL SURGEON

*E*dward Cree arrived in Hong Kong on HMS *Rattlesnake*, soon after the island became a British colony. Cree kept a journal. On 30 April 1841, he noted that he went ashore to see 'the new village which is springing up rapidly on Hong Kong'.

The British troops and merchants were living under canvas but 'a great influx of natives—ruffians from Canton—have erected huts and shanties, where are drinking booths and gambling booths and every kind of debauchery'. A few months later, malaria decimated the British.

When he returned in 1845, he 'walked through the town to see the new buildings, which are wonderful considering what Hong Kong was only two years ago'.

It was a time of fun and parties. He described how Lieutenant Dunlop of the Madras Native Infantry, who was 'dreadfully spoony with Miss Hickson', fell over and split his 'continuations' on a picnic. The belle of Hong Kong 'was so cruel as to laugh immoderately'.

Cree was invited to Government House, where he met 'a large party of bigwigs, but only got a poor dinner'. He witnessed Mr Justice Hulme's drunken hornpipe with the Mandarin Tung aboard HMS *Agincourt*.

Edward Cree was a Naval Surgeon. He was also an amateur artist and illustrated his journal lavishly with watercolours. He took part in Rajah Brooke's famous 1845 campaign against the pirates of Borneo.

The second time Cree came to the Far East was on the steam paddle sloop HMS *Fury*. Miss Hickson was now married. Cree went pirate hunting in Bias Bay and then took part in Captain Dalrymple Hay and General Wang Hai-quang's anti-pirate expedition to Hainan. At the height of the battle, General Wang jumped overboard and swam to a junk, which he captured single-handedly. The Anglo-Chinese fleet destroyed fifty-eight pirate junks.

Cree returned to England in 1850. He later fought in the Crimean War and was at the capture of Sebastopol.

A Chinese wedding, Ningbo. Watercolour by Edward Cree, 1844

Edward Cree's wood engraving of HMS Medea fighting pirates at Mirs Bay

Attack on the pirate squadron of Chui Apoo. Lithograph by Cree, 1849

44

CAPTAIN WILLIAM THORNTON BATE, RN
HYDROGRAPHER

Captain William Thornton Bate, RN, was an archetypal specimen of the Victorian muscular Christian. During the Opium War of 1839–42, he scaled the massive walls of Chapu alone and single-handedly captured the gates of the city.

Early in the battle he was engaged in a furious sword fight with a blue-button Mandarin, which ended up in a wrestling match on the ground. Bate, who was built like a bull, came out on top and history does not record how much weight the gallant Mandarin gave away to his massive, belligerent opponent.

In the balmy days of peace, Bate, in a tiny schooner called HMS *Starling*, surveyed Hong Kong waters and the coasts of China. Starling Inlet is named after his ship and Bate's Head after the man himself. He later spent four years charting the island of Palawan.

In spite of being a deeply religious man, he enjoyed nothing more than a good fight. During the Arrow War with China, which began in 1856, he defended the Macau Fort against enormous odds. This fort is not actually in Macau, but on an island in the Pearl River. It later became a leper colony and, much more recently, a duck farm.

Bate kept up the morale of his besieged troops by preaching them endless sermons on the evils of drink, swearing and the fleshpots of China: 'I fear that money, wine and women are the besetting sins of the majority of the foreign community in Canton,' he wrote.

Bate's reckless bravery under fire was legendary. Hong Kong's Colonial Chaplain wrote: 'The bullet was not cast which would kill Bate.' Bate was shot dead under the walls of Canton on 29 December 1857.

Captain Bate had loved visiting Hong Kong. After he died, a massive monument to his memory was erected by the citizens of the colony. Today, all that is left of this memorial is a rose-coloured stone set in the wall of St John's Cathedral. The monument, which survived the war, was destroyed by the Public Works Department when it widened Garden Road in the 1950s.

Captain William Thornton Bate, RN

Laurence Oliphant's drawing of the storming of Canton in 1857

John Thomson's magnificent photograph of Macau Fort

KEYING
CHINESE STATESMAN

The Ching Imperial Commissioner, Keying, first visited Hong Kong in 1843 to sign the Treaty of the Bogue. After the ceremony, the Governor, Sir Henry Pottinger, gave a splendid dinner at which Keying sang some Manchu songs. He was probably rather pleased with himself, because he had cunningly inserted into the Chinese text of the treaty a number of clauses favourable to China, which were not to be found in the English version. A few days later, when Pottinger discovered that he had been duped, he was completely flummoxed.

Keying liked a good party. He thoroughly enjoyed watching Hong Kong's Chief Justice, John Hulme, and the Manchu Mandarin, Tung, dance a wild hornpipe at a ball given in his honour aboard HMS *Agincourt*. When Hulme was later accused of being drunk, his defence was that his unsteady gait was due to varicose veins.

Keying had an eye for the ladies; at the same party he developed a morbid interest in Miss Hickson's bustle. In spite of his duplicity, Keying was very popular in Hong Kong. When a group of Hong Kong merchants bought a Chinese junk in Canton, they named it the *Keying* after the Commissioner. It was illegal in China to sell a junk to a foreigner. The offence was punishable by death, but nobody seemed to be particularly worried.

The voyage of the *Keying* to Europe is one of the great sea sagas of the age. The junk survived a hurricane off the Cape of Good Hope and eventually reached St Helena safely. The plan was to sail on directly to London, but the junk was blown off course. Captain Charles Kellet, with a near-mutinous crew on his hands, had to stop off at New York. After a voyage of 477 days the *Keying* finally arrived in London. Queen Victoria was among the thousands who visited the vessel, before this beautiful junk was broken up in order to sell her valuable teak planking for large sums of cash.

The Chinese junk, Keying

The cabin of the Keying

ELDRED POTTINGER
HERO OF HERAT

There was much speculation when Major Eldred Pottinger of the Bombay Regiment of Artillery arrived in the colony in 1843 to stay with his uncle, Sir Henry Pottinger, the first governor of Hong Kong. The rumour was that Eldred would succeed Sir Henry as governor.

Eldred, who was only thirty-three at the time, was known as the 'Hero of Herat'. Both uncle and nephew had been secret agents. Sir Henry, when twenty, had disguised himself as a Tartar horse trader and travelled 1,600 miles through Baluchistan, Afghanistan and Persia.

At times he pretended to be a holy man and had to bluff his way through a couple of religious debates. To convince a Baluchi village elder that you are a venerable Tartar *Hadji* when you have a thick Belfast accent requires a certain amount of the Blarney. They don't make governors like him anymore.

Thirty years later Eldred undertook a similar spying mission. He was in Herat when it was attacked by the Persians and Russians. Eldred immediately revealed his identity and took charge of the defence of the city. After ten months the Persians and Russians were forced to lift the siege and the road to British India was safe.

Major Eldred Pottinger

Eldred was wounded at the beginning of the First Afghan War and, with two other officers, was surrendered as a hostage during the ignominious British retreat from Kabul. This was a lucky break for him, because the ferocious Afghans massacred the rest of the British column of 16,000. Apart from the hostages, there was only one survivor. The plot of the book *Flashman*, by George MacDonald Fraser, is based loosely on his exploits.

Having survived the cannon balls of the Tsar of Russia and the daggers of Islam, the Hero of Herat proved no match for the Hong Kong mosquito. He died of malaria and is buried in an unmarked grave in Happy Valley cemetery.

Captain Hall's map of Hong Kong, 1844

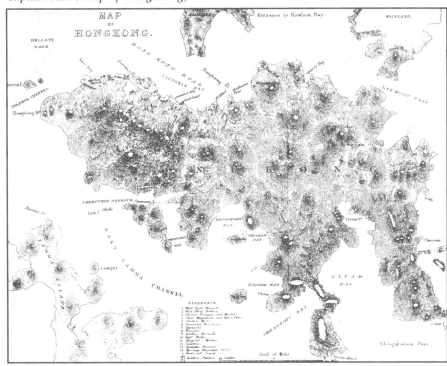

(following pages)
Happy Valley cemetery

GEORGE CHINNERY
ARTIST

~❦~

*I*n popular fiction George Chinnery is generally depicted as a loveable, garrulous, comic, stage Irishman who was wont to shout 'Begorra' or 'Bejabbers' at the twinkle of a leprechaun. He is often described as Hong Kong's greatest painter. Chinnery was English and London-born. He spent the last twenty-seven years of his life in Macau. He was over sixty-five years old when Sir Edward Belcher raised the Union Jack over Hong Kong. In reality, Chinnery did very few drawings of Hong Kong and he spent only six months in the colony at the end of 1845. He was basically a portrait painter, but is best known for the thousands of delightful little sketches of Canton and Macau.

Chinnery's painting of Macau

The Canton comprador, Howqua, by Chinnery

The studio of 'Lamqua, Handsome face painter'

George Chinnery was extremely ugly. He absconded to India to get away from his wife, who was even uglier than he was. After twenty years of happy separation, his wife turned up in Calcutta. She had not improved with age.

With the Chinese writer Shih Nai-an's famous maxim in mind—'Of the thirty-six ways of avoiding disaster, running away is best'—Chinnery fled to Macau and on to Canton. It was the ideal refuge. At that time foreigners were only allowed to stay in Canton if they obeyed a strict set of regulations. Chinnery rather liked the Draconian edict which, as he put it, 'forbids the softer sex from bothering us here'. At last, he had found a safe haven from his unloved wife.

Like many artists, when he was short of money Chinnery taught painting. Unfortunately, this backfired as gifted pupils like the Chinese artist Lamqua copied his style and drastically undercut his prices.

Chinnery's portrait of Assor, the Macau boatwoman

Lamqua set up a picture production line in Canton. One artist would paint the sky, another the sea, a third a junk...and so on. Outside the factory he hung a sign advertising 'Lamqua, Handsome face painter'. He charged only twenty-five silver dollars for a portrait. In 1852, at the age of seventy-eight, poor Chinnery died in poverty in his beloved Macau.

JOHN NEPTUNE SARGENT
IRISH SOLDIER

John Neptune Sargent was a man of violence, which is perhaps alright if you are a soldier. His ferocious temper was responsible for cutting short his stay in the colony on no less than two occasions.

In the last century, journalism was a perilous profession. The editors of the *Hongkong Daily Press*, the *Friend of China* and the *Hongkong Telegraph* all spent some time in gaol for libel. As what they wrote was sometimes true, their fines were often paid by public subscription. However, aggrieved readers occasionally took the law into their own hands. One of these was Lieutenant John Neptune Sargent of the 95th Regiment.

Before there was public street lighting in Hong Kong, every householder was required by law to have a lamp outside his door after nightfall. While on patrol, Lieutenant Sargent noticed that a lantern hanging outside a shop was not burning. The shopkeeper was taken to court. Unfortunately, when reporting the case, the editor of the *Hongkong Register*, Mr Cairns, referred to Sargent as an 'informer', not once but twice.

It is quite unwise to call an Irishman an informer. An infuriated Sargent descended like an avenging angel on poor Mr Cairns. He dragged the editor out of bed and 'struck him several blows on the head with his fist and umbrella'.

'You shall pay for this!' screamed Cairns; thereupon 'Sargent returned and gave Cairns a few more whacks with his umbrella'. On 6 December 1847, Sargent was fined $1,000 for assault. This discouraged the further horsewhipping of editors.

(following pages) *Thomas Allom's picture of a Chinese lantern shop*

Thirty-five years later, Sargent, now a Lieutenant-General, returned
to Hong Kong as the Commander of British Forces. The new General
was shocked by the colony's outdated artillery. Sargent wanted modern
guns. The Colonial Secretary, Lord Derby, instructed the Governor,
Sir George Bowen, to advance funds to pay for some howitzers. Bowen
foolishly questioned the instruction. Sargent lost his temper again.

Perhaps with Mr Cairns in mind, Bowen fled to Japan until the
General's fury abated. There, in the safety of the steam baths, he
sought a cure for a suspiciously convenient attack of rheumatism.

Victoria Barracks in Sargent's time

62

JAMES BODELL
BRITISH SOLDIER

In the middle of the last century Hong Kong was regarded by British soldiers as the most unsavoury posting in the world. The problem was malaria. Of the 650 men of the 59th Regiment, the 'Lillywhites', who landed in Hong Kong in 1850, only sixty-two remained two years later. One of them was Private James Bodell.

Bodell was so desperate that he tried to desert, but this was before Henry Hope Graham was made Colonel of the Lillywhites. Graham took over a decimated regiment. Under Graham it was more like belonging to a sports club than a fighting unit. Health and morale improved dramatically. Bodell was promoted to Sergeant and spent much of his time planting avenues of trees. Life was pleasant, but Bodell was still determined to leave. This cost money.

A comrade of Bodell's was an ex-Yarmouth fisherman who was an expert at network. They started a little net-making business. Bodell also did some sign-writing on the side and even experimented with hair-cutting.

Fortunately for Bodell, and unfortunately for the inhabitants of Hong Kong, a terrible fire broke out in Tai Ping Shan. With bulldog tenacity, the Lillywhites fought the conflagration. After the fire had burnt itself out, Bodell was given the job of preventing looting.

He describes in his reminiscences how 'at one time going around relieving Sentries and going amongst the Ruins I was ankle deep in Dollars'. There was, Bodell admitted, a certain amount of pilfering. For Bodell, it was a windfall.

The memorial to the 'Lillywhites' at Happy Valley

Bodell wanted to get married. He needed £18 to buy his discharge from the army and considerably more to set up business in the Australian colonies. For some inexplicable reason he chose Tasmania, where he bought a pub. He later worked in the goldfields, owned a few more pubs, drank the profits and went to New Zealand, where he fought in the Maori Wars. He finally sobered up and settled down there in Tauranga, where he manufactured lemonade and became Mayor.

The 59th Regiment of Foot at Hong Kong, by Charles Wirgman

The Hong Kong Fire Brigade in action

PRINCE WILLIAM OF HESSE
GERMAN ARISTOCRAT

*A*t the corner of Ice House Street and Zetland Street once stood the most beautiful classical building in Hong Kong. It was called Zetland Hall and was named after Thomas Dundas, Earl of Zetland, a Grand Master of the British freemasons.

It was built on the site of a small bungalow known as Tarantula Cottage, the home of William Tarrant, the venomous editor of the *Friend of China* newspaper.

In February 1853, His Highness Prince William of Hesse was in Hong Kong on a visit. Even in the last century princes were expected to do useful things like planting trees and kissing babies. The freemasons would have liked Prince William to lay the foundation stone of Zetland Hall, but the Grand Master of British Masons in China had already been asked to perform the ceremony.

Tarrant's *Friend of China* devoted a full page to the event. There was a splendid procession which included the bands of the 59th Regiment, and the US steam frigate *Susquehanna*. Brother Tarrant features rather prominently in the article in the *Friend of China* (which he wrote himself); although he only performed the humble role of reading out the inscription on the foundation stone before it was well and truly laid by the Grand Master. During the ceremony Prince William was entered as an apprentice.

Zetland Hall was designed by the Surveyor-General, Charles St George Cleverly, who was also the architect of the original Government House.

Zetland Hall

Cleverly seems to have been a rather more discriminating architect than he was a public servant.

The building was fondly known as 'The Bungalow' by the freemasons. Cleverly's magnificent Palladian portico, with its elegant Ionic and Doric columns, is sadly not reflected in the design of Hongkong Electric's substation that now stands on the site.

St George's House

68

LORD ELGIN
BRITISH PLENIPOTENTIARY

*J*ames Bruce, Earl of Elgin's father, became famous for looting the Elgin Marbles from the Parthenon in Athens. The cost of transporting the statues to England had almost bankrupted him. In order to restore the family fortune, his son went into public service.

When Lord Elgin arrived in Hong Kong in 1857, he had two objectives. The first was to establish a British Minister as an ambassador in Peking. The second was personal. At all costs he was determined to avoid staying at Government House as the guest of the Governor, Sir John Bowring, whom he loathed, despised and detested.

Lord Elgin signing the Treaty of Tientsin

The reception tent where the negotiations were conducted

Bowring had started an entirely unnecessary war with China over a minor incident concerning a lorcha called the *Arrow*. As a result of his actions, Lord Palmerston's Whig Government had been defeated in the House of Commons and was forced to resign.

Bowring had been stripped of his rank of British Plenipotentiary to the Court of Peking and the post had been given to Lord Elgin, who was sent to China to sort out the mess. Elgin decided to stay aboard HMS *Shannon*. It was unspeakably hot on board, but anything was better than Bowring.

He was later forced to change ships. The *Ava* was even hotter and, worse still, very smelly. Then Elgin discovered that his steward was storing onions below his cabin. 'Only conceive the abomination of such an arrangement', he moaned.

Elgin succeeded in persuading the Chinese Imperial Government to sign the Treaty of Tientsin. However, there were some problems when it came to ratification. These were sorted out in 1860 after he burned down the Summer Palace in Peking.

This act of barbarism made Elgin about as popular with the Chinese as his father is with the Greeks or his ancestor Robert the Bruce is with the English, whom he slaughtered by the thousands at the Battle of Bannockburn in 1314.

Elgin Street is named after him. There is speculation that the name will be changed after 1997.

CHARLES WIRGMAN
'SPECIAL ARTIST'

Charles Wirgman was sent by the *Illustrated London News* to China in 1857 to cover the Arrow War. He was a 'Special Artist'. As well as doing drawings and watercolours of the war, he was obliged to report on it as well. Today, this function would be performed by a photojournalist.

When Wirgman arrived in Hong Kong there was not very much going on. Although Britain and China were at war, there was little fighting. Wirgman did a few drawings of British troops camped on the Kowloon peninsula. He sent them back to London, where wood engravings were made from them. They were then printed in the *Illustrated London News*.

The Victorians used to bind copies of the magazine into volumes. These volumes—so lovingly collected—are now being bought up and ripped apart by vandalic picture dealers. The individual engravings are often hand coloured and sold off as 'original' prints. There are plenty of 'original' Wirgmans on sale in Hollywood Road and Cat Street today.

Unlike many of his contemporaries, Wirgman seemed to have thoroughly enjoyed the delights of the Orient:

> 'I am living at a Chinese house, and have a snug little room: no glass windows, a gorgeously carved bedstead—a regular Chinese one, on which I lay my mat. I order my breakfast in the dialect of Canton.

> 'I sometimes dine with a party of Chinese girls. I don't dislike their dinners at all. I eat and drink everything as they do; but as yet have not had the luck to taste puppy.

> 'The girls all want me to paint their likeness; and I have just painted my favourite in oils. She has been very kind to me, sends my clothes to wash, gets me sugar-cane, brings me cake, and otherwise treats me kindly.

> 'They have great objection to appear in the *Illustrated London News*. *'My no wantchee you puttee me dat lusee paper'*.

> 'Altogether, can I do otherwise than like Hong Kong?'

After the Arrow War Wirgman went to Japan, where he opened a photographic studio with the great photographer Felix Beato.

Wirgman's drawing of St John's Cathedral

CAPTAIN HENRY 'BULLY' HAYES
AMERICAN PIRATE

One-eared 'Bully' Hayes is reputed to have visited Hong Kong in 1857. Most books about Hong Kong pirates tell the tale of the capture of the notorious American pirate Eli Boggs by Bully Hayes, in a titanic struggle in the waters of Mirs Bay. The story goes that Boggs' pirate junk was cornered by two Royal Navy cutters. As the navy moved in, Boggs was seen to jump overboard. Shortly afterwards the junk exploded.

Bully, also an American, was aboard one of the cutters. He hurled himself into the water and swam in hot pursuit of the pirate. Being the stronger swimmer, Bully soon caught up with Boggs. With a howl of rage, Boggs stabbed at Bully with a wicked-looking knife. There was a sickening thud as Bully's iron fist connected with the bloodthirsty buccaneer's jaw.

For his gallantry in capturing Boggs, Bully received £1,000 reward. He also somehow managed to purloin two chests full of silver looted from one of Boggs' junks. This popular story was probably invented by Bully Hayes himself. As well as being a pirate, he was also a liar, a con man, a thief and a blackbirder.

At the time of Boggs' trial, Bully seems to have been in Australia preparing to commit bigamy for the second or third time with a young lady called Amelia Littleton. Boggs was actually arrested by a Constable Barker in Bonham Strand, Hong Kong. In his defence Boggs accused Ma Chow Wong, a bumboat proprietor, and a Police Magistrate, Daniel Caldwell, of being the real villains. Boggs was deported, Ma Chow Wong was transported and Caldwell was dismissed from service, after a monumental scandal that rocked the whole of Hong Kong.

As for the evil Bully—he roved the Pacific and the South China Sea for years, living a life of crime. He ended up being beaten to death by his sea cook, Dutch Pete, with a wooden 'boom crutch' (whatever that may be) and fed to the fishes off Jaluit Island.

Eli Boggs the pirate

74

A Chinese pirate junk

A fleet of Chinese pirates preparing to attack

GEORGE WINGROVE COOKE
JOURNALIST

George Wingrove Cooke arrived in 'British China' (as he called Hong Kong) on 22 May 1857. Cooke was the foreign correspondent of *The Times* newspaper. 'The Thunderer' had sent him out to cover the Arrow War in China. His arrival coincided with the phoney period of the war, when neither the Chinese Imperial Commissioner Yeh nor the British had sufficient power to do much more than growl at each other.

Victoria Harbour in Cooke's day

In his early dispatches Cooke tends to glamorize the danger of living in Hong Kong. He explains how everyone went around armed with a revolver because Commissioner Yeh had put a price of $500 on every European head delivered to his *yamen* in Canton. Although a few unfortunate drunks lost their heads, Hong Kong's ever-busy entrepreneurs harvested most of their grim crop from newly-dug graves in Happy Valley Cemetery.

Cooke's early dispatches tended towards the romantic. 'British China' reminded Cooke of a sort of Loch Lomond peopled by 'merchant princes living in many gorgeous palaces with every home luxury except a bracing breeze'. Cooke blithely misinformed his readers that the staple diet of the Chinese was steamed rat.

Cooke witnessed the capture of Canton. He left China aboard HMS *Inflexible* on 20 February 1858. The ship was carrying Commissioner Yeh, as a prisoner, to Calcutta. Cooke's later dispatches to *The Times* read today as a rather pathetic, schoolboyish attempt to turn Yeh into some sort of monstrous Oriental bogeyman. He no longer had much good to say about 'British China' either. In 1859 he wrote: 'Hong Kong is always connected with some fatal pestilence, some doubtful war, or some discreditable internal squabble, so much so that, in popular language, the name of this noisy, bustling, quarrelsome, discontented little Island may not inaptly be used as euphemous synonym for a place not mentionable to ears polite'.

He had certainly come a long way from the bonny, bonny banks of Loch Lomond.

The British factories at Canton

Commisioner Yeh

WILLIAM BLAKENEY
BRITISH HYDROGRAPHER

~~~~~~

William Blakeney was a man of unshakeable prejudices. He loved dogs, bears, sailing ships, German missionaries, Kipling, England and the Japanese. He hated monkeys, women, Russians and Hong Kong.

He arrived in the colony in 1857 aboard HMS *Actaeon*, after 232 days at sea. The *Actaeon* was an ancient survey vessel and her mission was to chart 'the coasts of Corea and Tartary, or the off-lying islands where the British Flag does not fly'. Unfortunately, the Arrow War was going on at the time and it was two years before 'Noah's Ark' began her mission.

It was unbearably hot aboard the ship: 'We were in a perpetual state of stew, and maddened by prickly heat.' His one relaxation was an early morning walk on shore and a swim.

The only way to get ashore was by a sampan 'womaned by Chinese'. At the time Commissioner Yeh, the Viceroy of Canton, was offering rewards for Englishmen's heads: 'The lady, tiller in hand, acted as a coxswain, and so, seated behind you, could at a suitable moment, if your vigilance was relaxed, deal you a stunning blow on the head.'

The flag which decorated Blakeney's Christmas pudding in 1858

These were dangerous times. When invited to a party at Government House, the Governor, Sir John Bowring, advised Blakeney to 'wear your sword, carry a loaded pistol, and keep your wits about you, coming up here in the dark!'.

When later they surveyed the Yangtze, an English name was given to every feature of the river. Blakeney was particularly gratified when a beautiful stretch of river was named 'Blakeney Reach' after him.

On Christmas Day 1858, they anchored somewhere near a nameless island. During the Christmas festivities the Captain's dog went berserk and bit eight sailors. The poor animal died, but achieved immortality when Captain Ward named the island after his canine shipmate. It seems that poor old Rover had rabies. 'Rover Island' is probably the only place in China which has the distinction of being named after a rabid maritime Irish retriever.

William Blakeney in naval uniform

The officers of HMS Actaeon

THE WAR IN CHINA.

SAMPAN GIRL ON CANTON RIVER.

engagement of the day was the capture of sundry geese, but they were duly paid for. The trumpet sounds, the men spring to their legs, and the aborigines take to their heels, leaving the ground clear for the homeward march.

I send you a portrait from the river—a Sampan Girl. I took this from nature a few days ago. It will give you an idea of how the women row: they always sit sideways. She wears her hair "à la teapot," as we call it here: it is very becoming, but takes some time to fix.

Next is a Josshouse—Tae Ping Shan—the finest one here, and into which I went the other day. I never shall forget the sight. Two women were paying their devotions; but in such a manner! Directly we came in they began laughing with us; then they bowed their foreheads on the floor; then they played tricks with each other, such as breaking little bits off the mat they were kneeling on, and putting them into one

ORDER OF MERIT OR VALOUR, JUST INSTITUTED BY YEH.

another's hair: one actually got up and lit her cigarette at the taper that was burning for joss. As for devotion, there was not an attempt made. The cigarette-woman went ahead, smoking, playing, and praying. A priest in a yellow gown was chanting at his litany, but was not unmindful of what was going on. Persons were walking about talking, and one man was tossing up a baby. Then the hideous gods—enough to give one the nightmare! We left the ladies and went to a shop opposite, where I sat down to make a sketch, but was so completely surrounded by Chinamen that it was a case of drawing under difficulties. The fellows are so fond of anything in the shape of a picture that one runs a risk of suffocation if he attempts out-door sketching. They don't mean to get in your way, but then they will imagine they are transparent. However, I made the sketch. On the steps are coolies, and immediately in front of each joss lion are peripatetic venders of yak fan edibles.

I have sketched also "The Crew of a Gun-boat at Prayers." This is Sunday morning in Canton River. The Captain is reading the service, and the tars, sitting on handspikes, are listening. In the background is part of North Wantong Fort. The canary-bird in the cage makes the scene appear quite domestic.

I send, also, a sketch of the Order of Valour just issued by Yeh: it is of silver, and larger than the sketch.

(Continued from page 169.)

In the meantime Yeh remains stubborn, and we cannot help admiring his pluck and endurance. The Portrait I send you may be relied upon, being copied from the painting of a native artist of great merit. It is generally believed that the Chinese have removed their goods and chattels from the city, and have undermined it considerably, with a view to the blowing up as many Fanqui as possible, Yeh himself superintending *in propriâ personâ*. I hope in my next to give you an account of our successful destruction of all its defences and the occupation of the city. The principal, indeed the only, amusement is a walk on shore—every one armed, of course. The other day the *Nankin* sent a walking party on a grand scale—nearly 300 men. Having arrived at a suitable spot, we proceeded, Fanqui fashion, to restore the inner man: the never-failing tribe of rags and tatters crowded round as usual. The band struck up, "In the days when we went gipsying," "Polly won't you try me, oh?" and other airs of an exhilarating tendency. The Celestials formed a complete hedge, the small boys in front, and others bringing up the rear. Our "brave army," stretched on the grass, enjoyed itself freely. As far as the eye could reach, turnips met our view, and refreshed our men. The only

JOSSHOUSE (TAE PING SHAN) AT CANTON.

London: Printed and Published at the Office, 198, Strand, in the Parish of St. Clement Danes, in the County of Middlesex, by WILLIAM LITTLE, 198, Strand, aforesaid.—SATURDAY, FEBRUARY 13, 1858.

A page of the Illustrated London News, 13th February 1858

ALBERT SMITH
ENTERTAINER

At the age of thirty-five Albert Smith climbed Mont Blanc, thus achieving his life's ambition. He spent the next seven years talking about it. His one-man show, *Mr Albert Smith's Ascent of Mont Blanc*, was a great success. It was a half-serious, half-humorous lecture on mountaineering, interspersed with comic songs and witty stories about the way Englishmen behaved abroad.

He was in Hong Kong in the summer of 1858 to collect material for a new show, *Mont Blanc to China*. He visited the notorious American pirate Eli Boggs in gaol. Smith describes Boggs as 'very good looking, with long dark hair, and a very remarkable eye, almost round, with a large pupil like a black bead'.

Albert Smith

Boggs' great enemy, Daniel Caldwell—who held the post of 'Protector of the Chinese'—took Smith 'for a prowl about the low quarters'. This was before Caldwell was convicted for owning brothels. It was a time of unspeakable corruption in the colony. All Smith wanted to do was to pick up a few interesting Chinese curios and a bit of local colour for his new show, but the British community was far too busy quarrelling to be of much help.

82

Hongkong, China
Victoria Street

cher Mo...
Depinchart.
Tout marche
encore bien
encore 1 escale
et n: partons
ps Tientsin
les complim...
à votre dame
Bien à vous

Sten...Co., Dre...c 12501

A postcard of the first Hong Kong Club

Fortunately, he was introduced to Rafael Rozario, a law court interpreter. Thanks to Rozario, Smith became an instant expert on China and everything Chinese: Cantonese opera, chopsticks, birds' nests and shark fin soup. Among the artefacts he collected was a lump of the famous poisoned bread—a keepsake from the plot to murder the European population of Hong Kong the previous year. He bought Chinese lanterns, mandarins' robes, fans and tiny 'golden lily' shoes—anything that would titillate the imagination of Victorian London. He hired a local artist, M A Baptista, to design the scenery for the show.

Smith was in Hong Kong for just over a month. His new show opened in time for Christmas; it was a huge success.

WALTER WHITE
PAINTER 1ST CLASS, RN

Chinese New Year in Hong Kong is much quieter than it was in Walter White's time. White was a painter aboard HMS *Scout*, a wooden screw corvette of the Pearl Class. He spent the Lunar New Year of 1862 on shore leave at the European Hotel, which overlooked the Chinese quarter of Tai Ping Shan. From the veranda of his hotel he could look down and observe how the average Chinese spent the holiday. His conclusion was that the 'sole enjoyment on that day is crackers'.

'In order to understand you must bear in mind that a Chinese cracker is not a thing to be trifled with. It is a slab about an inch in thickness, four inches wide and any length you please. It goes off with a bang, each as loud as that of a gun, hops about from one side of the street to the other, flying ten or twelve feet unforeseen into the air.' White did not get much sleep during his shore leave: 'Every door contained a party letting off these diabolical preparations.'

The Chinese have long used fire crackers to 'put to flight the fell and foul spirits that love to lurk about the haunts of men. Therefore at all joyous events such as marriages, processions, Saint's days and feasts, immunity from ill has to be purchased by their explosion'. The practice of letting off fireworks on every 'joyous' occasion in Hong Kong ceased abruptly in August 1967, during disturbances caused by the Cultural Revolution in China. There is now no reason why the ban

An alley in the Chinese quarter of Hong Kong

84

should not be lifted, as no self-respecting terrorist would dream of using an explosive as primitive as gunpowder to manufacture a bomb.

But the traditional pyrotechnics has proved an unnecessary expense which the average citizen of Hong Kong could do without, so the ban still remains in force. Anyhow, nowadays the 'fell and foul spirits that love to lurk about the haunts of men' are far too sophisticated to be terribly impressed by a few bangs.

A Tai Ping Shan street

Victoria Harbour in the 1860s

HRH DUKE OF EDINBURGH
FIRST ROYAL VISITOR

Prince Alfred, Duke of Edinburgh, had planned to visit the colony in 1868. Unfortunately, his visit was delayed for a year. This was because he went to Australia first, where Herbert O'Farrell, an Irishman, shot him in the back. The bullet hit the joint of his sturdy navy braces, which saved his life. He spent a year convalescing before renewing his royal tour. He arrived in Hong Kong aboard HMS *Galatea* on 31 October 1869.

Affie, as Queen Victoria called her sailor son, landed with great pomp and splendour: 'All the Men-of-War in the Harbour, British and Foreign were now wreathed in the folds of a sulphurous canopy, as, in concert with the Shore Battery, they thundered forth together the Royal Salute'. Two American sailors were injured in this artillery barrage. Affie gave them £50 before he left Hong Kong.

Prince Alfred had few official functions to attend. He opened the new City Hall and laid the foundation stone for the choir at St John's Cathedral. He spent most of his time refitting his ship and watching amateur theatricals. There was a splendid production of a comedy called *Notting Hill*. The *China Mail* reported how the heroine, Lizzy, comforted Policeman X 'in a way which is supposed to be peculiarly agreeable to the frequenters of our streets'. The hero was a Private Tight-Leather. It all sounds rather daring stuff for Victorian Hong Kong.

The street decorations were magnificent, the banquets sumptuous and

Prince Alfred, Duke of Edinburgh

the speeches flattering. The Duke was presented with a
nine-foot, Chinese satin scroll, embroidered in gold with five-clawed
dragons. It described him as 'Fair as the plumes of Phoenix, that sits
in the crimson nest; Graceful as a Unicorn, auspiciously nurtured on
the sombre hills'. How times have changed. During the second official
visit, by Queen Elizabeth II in 1986, the present Duke of Edinburgh,
Prince Philip, was given a stuffed pied kingfisher by the World Wide
Fund for Nature.

Royal visit street decorations

The City Hall, which was opened by the Duke of Edinburgh

The Praya at the time of the royal visit

The arrival of the Duke of Edinburgh at Pedder Wharf

The Hong Kong Club illuminated with Chinese lanterns

SARA DELANO
MOTHER OF A PRESIDENT

'Nothing, like something, happens anywhere,' wrote the British poet, Philip Larkin. Sometimes when nothing happens, or something doesn't happen, the whole course of history can be changed.

Sara Delano with her son, Franklin Delano Roosevelt, later the President of the United States of America

When Sara Delano visited her family in Hong Kong in 1876, absolutely nothing happened— but it almost did. There was a shortage of twenty-two-year-old American beauties in the colony at the time and Sara was ardently courted by a young man who eventually asked her to marry him.

Her family did not approve of her suitor and instructed her to reject his proposal. She returned to New York unmarried. History does not reveal who her *inamorato* was or why he was considered unsuitable. Perhaps he was a Democrat. Sara's father, Warren Delano Jr, was paranoiac about Democrats. His political philosophy is best summed up in his statement, 'I will not say that all Democrats are horse thieves, but it does seem that all horse thieves are Democrats'.

Warren Delano Jr was a swashbuckling adventurer and drug runner of the old school. He worked for Russell and Company before the Opium War, when they were the largest American dealers in 'foreign mud' in Canton. He was a clipper captain and later became a partner of the

92

The Opium Trade

firm. At one time he was the American vice-consul in Canton.

In 1850, he opened up a branch office of Russell and Company in Hong Kong with George Tyson. His fortune made, he took his family back to New York, but in 1859 he was on the verge of bankruptcy so he returned to Hong Kong, where he made a second opium fortune.

At twenty-six Sara was still unmarried, when she met James Roosevelt. He proposed to her. In spite of being a Democrat, Warren considered him a gentleman and the couple were married in 1880. Their first child was born two years later. They named the baby Franklin Delano Roosevelt. He later became the thirty-second President of the United States of America. He was also a Democrat.

SIR HUGH LOW
NATURALIST

Sir Hugh Low was one of those strange creatures who enjoyed nothing more than to live in the middle of the jungle, miles from anywhere, talking to plants, birds, butterflies and fruit trees. In 1877, he was appointed British Resident in Perak. Low kept a small gibbon called Elbis. Elbis used to open his mail and pretend to read it. One morning he discovered Elbis sitting at his breakfast table, totally engrossed in a letter from Low's daughter Kitty. It was a cry for help.

Kitty was married to the Governor of Hong Kong, the tempestuous Sir John Pope Hennessy. The Governor had disturbed Kitty and Judge Hayllar in her boudoir, poring over a catalogue of the *Museo Borbonica* in Naples. Hennessy accused the judge of trying to seduce Kitty with filthy pictures. A few days later, Sir John attempted to 'horsewhip' Hayllar with his umbrella in a confrontation on the Peak. The judge was much larger than Sir John, whose small son refused to let go of his hand during the affray. Sir John was disarmed by Hayllar, who hung the umbrella above his mantelpiece as a trophy.

Kitty Pope Hennessy

(previous pages)
Opium ships at Lintin Island, 1824, by W J Huggins

Sir Hugh Low loathed his son-in-law. Low had expected to be appointed Governor of Labuan, where he had served for years, but the British government had given the job to Hennessy instead. Soon afterwards Hennessy had married Kitty, then seventeen years old. On arrival, in response to Kitty's letter, Low refused to stay at Government House and moved into the Hong Kong Hotel. He instantly made friends with Hayllar and persuaded him to withdraw his complaint to the Secretary of State about the Governor's outrageous behaviour. In spite of Low's efforts, the incident developed into a monstrous scandal.

Having failed in his mission, Sir Hugh Low returned to the tranquility of Perak, where he planted and lovingly nurtured the first rubber trees in Malaya. This was the humble beginning of the mighty Malaysian rubber industry.

Tapping rubber in Malaya

The Hong Kong Hotel on the waterfront

Mountain Lodge, where Sir John caught Judge Hayller showing Kitty 'filthy pictures'

GENERAL
ULYSSES S GRANT
AMERICAN PRESIDENT

The ex-President of the United States, General Ulysses S Grant, stopped off in Hong Kong for three days in May 1879. The General was welcomed by the Governor, Sir John Pope Hennessy, and local dignitaries.

It had been planned that the highlight of his visit was to be a magnificent open-air party in the Botanical Gardens. A Triumphal Arch had been built, which was to be illuminated by gaslight, with a transparency of the General on one side and the flags of Great Britain and the United States on the other. The band of the 27th Regiment was on hand to play a selection of waltzes. There was to be a magnificent display of fireworks. On the morning of the party, which was a Saturday, the weather was windy. The Organising Committee panicked. They summoned the manager of the gas company, who assured them confidently that, as the lights were protected by glass globes, they had nothing to worry about.

The Governor had promised to throw open Government House if the weather was bad, but the Organising Committee didn't take up his offer. Instead, they postponed the party until the following Monday. Circulars were issued informing the public of the change of time. Unfortunately, nobody had bothered to check when General Grant was leaving the colony. The *Zambesi*, with the General aboard, steamed out of harbour twelve hours before the great 'Welcome to Hong Kong General Grant Party' began.

The *China Mail* was particularly scathing about the blunder: 'General Grant will have to credit the Hong Kong community with an embryonic reception, while it contained the elements of heartiness and sincerity, was strangled at birth by a lack of organization, and a plethora of mismanagement, which unfortunately are usual characteristics of semi-public efforts of this Colony'.

General Ulysses S Grant,
President of
the United States.
Photograph
by Matthew Brady

The Triumphal Arch in the
Botanical Gardens

Grant triumphal Arch, Erected to welcome the arrival of General
Grant, the American President, in his visit to Hongkong in 1874

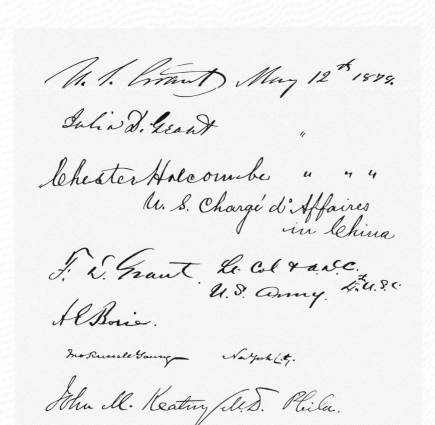

A page from a Government House Visitors Book, featuring Grant's signature

ISABELLA BIRD
PROFESSIONAL TRAVELLER

*I*sabella Bird was one of those indomitable Victorian lady-travellers
who bravely tramped around some of the most disease-ridden places
in the East in order, she explained, 'to recruit my health'.

Her curiosity for the unusual was insatiable. During a visit in early
1879, she persuaded her host Dr Burdon, the Bishop of Hong Kong,
to show her the prison.

The Governor, Sir John Pope Hennessy, was particularly proud of
his prison reforms. Against strong local opposition, he had forbidden
flogging and branding and improved the living conditions of convicts.
Miss Bird thought he had gone a little too far. Writing to her sister in
Edinburgh she explained that: 'The accommodation, food, etc., are as
much superior to the houses and manner of living of the poorer Chinese
as our rooms and way of living in Atholl Crescent are superior to that of
the dwellers of Cowgate'.

She was not impressed by Sir John: 'It strikes me that he is posing
as an humanitarian...The prison pleased me, but Governor Hennessy
obviously has a diseased sympathy with criminals'.

Perhaps she was right. During Hennessy's governorship there was a
massive crime wave. This resulted in a demonstration against his re-

The public flogging post

102

Isabella Bird

forms by almost the entire European community on the cricket ground
in October 1878.

There was a counter-demonstration in support of the Governor by the
local Chinese, who sent an address to Queen Victoria expressing confi-
dence in Hennessy. After sitting on the problem for over a year, the
British Government confirmed most of the Governor's reforms.
Hennessy's ability to divide a community is legendary. His policies
caused riots and unrest in almost every colony he governed. On the whole
Hong Kong got off lightly. 'I hope the Governor will be recalled,' wrote
Isabella Bird. Most of the European community agreed with her.

HENRY
PRINCE OF PRUSSIA

*I*n May 1880, the younger brother of the future Kaiser Wilhelm II, Prince Henry of Prussia, sailed into Hong Kong aboard his ship the *Prince Albert*. Unwittingly he found himself in the centre of a storm.

It was not a typhoon but a gigantic row between the Governor, Sir John Pope Hennessy, and the Commander of British Forces, Major-General E W Donovan. The quarrel between the two cantankerous Irishmen was originally over sanitation and land usage, but the feud soon got completely out of hand.

The General refused to speak to the Governor or to attend Executive Council meetings. He would not allow a military band to play at the Queen's Birthday Party at Government House. Instead he organized his own Queen's Birthday Party in competition to the Governor's.

Prince Henry offered, rather naïvely, to lend the Governor his ship's band. Hennessy was delighted and invited Prince Henry, who was staying at Government House, to co-host the dinner. This was an appalling breach of protocol and caused a storm in London. Eventually, the War

British troops on parade in Hong Kong

Office instructed the General to provide the Governor with a band.

The feud raged on. Hennessy had stopped building reservoirs, because he claimed they were against Chinese tradition, and was violently opposed to the introduction of flush toilets to the colony.

Donovan reported Hennessy's antics to the Colonial Surgeon, who sent over Osbert Chadwick to investigate the sanitary conditions of Hong Kong. This resulted in the Chadwick Report, which was to become the cornerstone of Hong Kong's health policy.

Prince Henry spent most of his time wandering around Hong Kong incognito, avoiding the Governor, with his 'minder', Baron Seckendorff, in tow.

The Governor, in spite of being a former Irish Nationalist Tory Member of Parliament, loved royalty and attempted to create a 'royal occasion' by persuading his guest to unveil a picture of the Prince Consort. Baron Seckendorff intervened, however. In the end, a compromise was reached whereby the Governor unveiled the portrait and Prince Henry reluctantly made a short speech.

Sir John Pope Hennessy

KING DAVID KALAKAUA
KING OF THE HAWAIIAN ISLANDS

ing David Kalakaua passed through Hong Kong in April 1881 on his famous round-the-world royal tour. In Hawaii he was known as the 'Merry Monarch' and the ruler of the 'Champagne Dynasty', but his visit to the colony was far from merry.

There had been speculation in the local newspapers as to where

King Kalakaua and Sir John Pope Hennessy

Kalakaua; of the Hawaiian Islands, King.
Government House
Hong Kong April 21st 1881.

the King was going to stay during his visit. The Hawaiian Consul in Hong Kong, William Keswick, who was a Legislative Councillor and the taipan of Jardines, had invited him to stay at his house at East Point but, when the Governor, Sir John Pope Hennessy, heard about this, he insisted that the King should stay at Government House.

There was a race between Keswick and the Governor's Private Secretary, Dr Eitel, to meet the King's ship, which Keswick won by a short head. Keswick tactfully suggested as a compromise that King Kalakaua would spend the first night at his home and the rest of his visit at Government House. Eitel would not agree and there was an unseemly row. Eventually, the King decided that it would be more diplomatic to accept the Governor's invitation.

As a result of the quarrel, the Governor excused himself from Keswick's garden party but his wife, Kitty, went along. Unfortunately, so did Judge Hayllar, whom the Governor suspected of being her lover. They were photographed together. Kitty tried to have the picture suppressed, but she was too late—the photographer, A Fong, had already sold a number of prints.

King Kalakaua, who was a man of the world, does not seem to have been upset by the petty squabbles which marred his visit. He probably enjoyed a little scandal. Before becoming king, this easy-going monarch had been a newspaper editor.

GENERAL CHARLES GORDON
COMMANDER OF THE EVER-VICTORIOUS ARMY

In the final years of the Taiping Rebellion of 1851–64, the citizens of Shanghai raised an army to protect them from the rebels. The Ever-Victorious Army was a rabble of mercenaries, deserters, sailors, looters and drunks when Major Charles Gordon of the Royal Engineers took command in 1863. He soon beat them into shape. Under Gordon the army fought thirty-three battles and played a positive part in putting down the rebellion. Gordon was made a Mandarin and given a yellow jacket. He left China a hero.

Gordon did not return to China for another seventeen years. He spent most of the time in between putting down the slave trade in the Sudan. China was having trouble with Imperial Russia at the time. There were two parties in Peking: the Peace Party of Prince Kung and Li Hung-chang (who was Gordon's old colleague from the Taiping Rebellion days) and the War Party of Princes Chun and Tso. The War Party wanted China to invade Russia. As China did not stand a chance against the military might of the Tsar, Gordon wisely advised them against going to war. Before he left China, Gordon wrote a manifesto advising the Chinese on how to fight the Russians should the need arise. This document bears a remarkable resemblance to a book by

General Gordon

108

Prince Kung

Chairman Mao Tse-tung, published many years later and called
Basic Tactics.

The noble Gordon refused to accept any payment for his services to
China. As a result he arrived in Hong Kong penniless and had to get a
loan from the Hongkong and Shanghai Bank. He stayed with the
Governor, Sir John Pope Hennessy. They seemed to have got on rather
well; which is surprising, as it would be difficult to find two more
prickly, arrogant, autocratic and quarrelsome megalomaniacs.

There was still trouble in the Sudan: the Mahdi had massacred
Hicks Pasha's army and Gordon was sent there to sort out the mess. His
instructions were to evacuate Khartoum, which was under siege. Gordon
typically refused to budge. On 26 January 1885, the Mahdi swept into
Khartoum and slaughtered the former commander of the Ever-Victorious
Army.

'Chinese Gordon' in mandarin robes

The artillery of the Ever-Victorious Army

C.G. Gordon. 8 July. 1880.

P G WODEHOUSE
COMIC WRITER

P G Wodehouse was the son of a superintendent in the Hong Kong Police, who named his son Pelham Grenville after Colonel Pelham Grenville von Donop, a Hong Kong friend. Pelham was generally known as 'Plum' by his family and friends.

In 1881, his father was promoted to Police Magistrate and Coroner. When he retired in 1898 a local newspaper remarked that: 'He was perhaps more known for his gentlemanliness and conscientiousness than for his brilliant finesse; but, when he made a mistake, he was ever ready to own it and seek to remedy it'.

Wodehouse sent his children to England. When Plum left school he joined the London branch of the Hongkong and Shanghai Bank. He turned out to be about as capable a banker as his father was a magistrate. He wrote: 'There were only two things connected with Higher Finance that I really understood. One was that from now on all I would be able to afford by way of lunch would be a roll and butter and a cup of coffee, a discovery which, after the lavish midday meals of school, shook me to the foundations. The other was that if I got to the office late three mornings in a month, I would lose my Christmas bonus'.

After two years of 'Higher Finance' he left the Bank to become a full-time writer: 'The thought of being a branch manager appalled me, for I knew myself incapable of managing a whelk-stall.'

Hong Kong is not strong on literary celebrities. Although he was not born in the Colony, he has sometimes been described as one of Hong Kong's most famous sons. There have also been wild theories that Bertie Wooster and Jeeves were based on characters he had known in Hong Kong. This is unlikely. P G Wodehouse spent only a few months in Hong Kong. He was two years old at the time.

The Hongkong and Shanghai Bank, Queen's Road

A Chinese police constable

Sikh policemen guarding criminals in stocks

PRINCE ALBERT VICTOR AND PRINCE GEORGE
SAILOR PRINCES

Queen Victoria's grandsons, Prince Albert Victor and Prince George, arrived in Hong Kong aboard HMS *Bacchante* on 20 December 1881. There were strict instructions that the Princes should be treated merely as junior naval officers and not as royal visitors. The Governor, the snobbish Sir John Pope Hennessy, ignored this directive, which infuriated the Admiral, Lord Clanwilliam. The decorations were magnificent. It was reported that 'the illuminations in front of the Hongkong and Shanghai Bank were exceedingly well got up', Kelly & Walsh's illuminations on their bookshop were described as 'chaste', while the *Hongkong Telegraph* claimed that its own decorations inspired 'admiration and awe' and poured scorn on the feeble efforts of its rival, the *China Mail*.

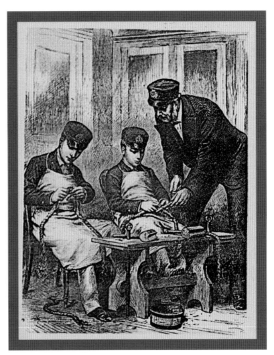

The sailor princes splicing rope aboard HMS Bacchante

Everything did not run smoothly. General Donovan's Royal Inniskilling Fusiliers pelted a loyal Chinese procession with rubbish as it passed Murray Barracks. Hennessy organized a Government House Ball in honour of the Princes; but the Admiral, probably out of spite, refused to let them attend. However, the Princes were allowed to go to the Public Subscription Ball on New Year's Eve.

The highlight of the visit was the regatta and a race between the man-of-war cutters, where HMS *Bacchante* thrashed a crew from the Admiral's ship HMS *Iron Duke*: 'Prince George's crew pulled well together, gamely responding to the vigorous calls of the coxswain, and drew clear in the last 300 yards.'

The Royal Engineers' racing gig during the regatta

Murray Barracks

There were numerous games of cricket. Lord Harris, the captain of Essex, hit a magnificent 102 runs for the Hong Kong Club against the Officers of the Army and Navy and the Middlesex bowler I D Walker's 'underhand twisters demoralized even the best bats'. The Hong Kong Club won.

Prince George later became King George V. His elder brother, Prince Albert Victor, who was somewhat 'backward', died in 1892. There was a nasty rumour that Prince Albert was Jack the Ripper, the notorious Whitechapel mass murderer.

116

A page of the Illustrated London News, showing Hong Kong festivities in honour of the sailor princes

COUNT POPOW
CONFIDENCE TRICKSTER

There is something truly romantic about a man who tries to sail round the world, particularly when he is a charming Russian nobleman and the sole survivor of a ghastly shipwreck. It is great newspaper material. The *China Mail* recorded how 'Count Popow burst with the suddenness of a new star upon the small world of Hong Kong'.

Popow claimed that his private yacht, the *Cooslie Doo*, had been wrecked near Pulo Obi and, after some hair-raising adventures, he had reached Bangkok. It was such an absurd story that the gullible public believed it and, for a few months in 1888, Popow was the darling of Hong Kong society.

His new friends feasted and fêted him and lent him money. There was consternation in the Hong Kong Club when it was discovered that 'he was strutting in borrowed plumes and that he had no more claim to the title of a Russian Count than a street coolie'.

A few years after his release from Victoria Gaol he reappeared in Mauritius, resplendent in the gorgeous uniform of a French admiral. Vice Admiral Wilsen (as he then called himself) did rather better in Mauritius than Count Popow had done in Hong Kong. While he was waiting for his flagship, he lived in lavish style in a splendid villa on the most fashionable part of the island and was frequently invited to dine at Government House.

As he did in Hong Kong, Popow lingered a little too long. His illusive flagship never appeared. But instead of borrowing money from the business community, the cunning Popow ruthlessly milked the consular corps. When at last he was exposed, these gentlemen were too embarrassed to prosecute. Consequently, they were not very happy when Popow's brilliant uniform appeared on a tailor's dummy in the window of the local shop of the Singer Sewing Machine Company, together with an inscription which told the whole sordid story.

The Hong Kong Club, where Count Popow spent time

Victoria Gaol, where Count Popow 'did time'

GERALDINE GUINNESS
MISSIONARY

In March 1888, Miss Geraldine Guinness arrived in Hong Kong. 'It is wonderful,' she wrote. 'We are inundated with Chinese.' She headed straight for the Sailors' Home.

Geraldine Guinness

'It was a happy little gathering of some sixty or eighty men—rough sailor fellows and others, sitting in the bright, homelike room, just like our men in Bromley.' When Miss Guinness asked if anyone came from the East End of London, 'quite a number held up horny, brown hands!'. Mr Goldsmith of the Gospel Temperance Society then lectured the horny-handed sailor fellows on the evils of drink.

Miss Guinness was a missionary. Her father, Henry Grattan Guinness, was the author of a famous Victorian hymn on China, 'The Voice of Thy Brother's Blood'. His message was simple: 'A million a month in China are dying—without God!' He had sent his daughter Geraldine to the East to rectify this unfortunate situation.

The China Inland Mission tended to employ single women. In 1888 they had 316 missionaries in China. They had a dismal ratio of eight communicants per missionary, whereas the Canadian Presbyterians came top with 265 converts each.

W Somerset Maugham, writing fifty years later, gives the impression that the Protestant missionaries in China lived off the fat of the land, but this was not true of pioneers like little Miss Guinness. Judging by her letters, she seems to have survived on rice, tea and hard-boiled eggs, although one Christmas dinner on the Ha River was more exciting: 'Rice, potatoes, carrots, tea and bread—why, we are well-off, indeed!'

Miss Guinness seldom complained about life in China. Sometimes the dirt and squalor became too much even for her indomitable spirit, but she was a cheerful little soul who tended to see the bright side of life: 'Keating's insect powder is most comforting, happily we have some with us', she wrote from a 'filthy, odoriferous' inn suppurating in the 'Heart of Heathendom'.

The Lord's Prayer

A pamphlet published by the
Chinese Religious Tract Society

'Come over and help us'. A Chinese scroll

MARIE-CHARLES DAVID DE MAYRENA
KING OF THE SEDANGS

It is sometimes difficult to define the difference between the unsuccessful adventurer and the con man, but one thing is certain: Hong Kong's obvious wealth has always attracted this type of visitor.

When the 'King of the Sedangs' arrived in the Colony in November 1888 on a fund-raising trip, the hard-nosed taipans were not very impressed, but he was amusing and they were prepared to listen. If an English army officer, James Brooke, had managed to establish himself as the 'White Rajah' amongst the wild head-hunters of Sarawak, why shouldn't a French officer do the same thing in the more civilized Indochina?

Unlike Brooke, the King wore gorgeous uniforms of fantastical design and generously awarded decorations to his cronies, who hung around the bar of the Hong Kong Hotel where he was staying. His attempts to raise money from the Roman Catholic Church suffered a setback when the 'Queen of the Sedangs', a Swedish blonde, arrived and moved into an apartment in Lyndhurst Terrace, the upmarket brothel area of the colony.

De Mayréna aroused the anger of Murray Bain, the editor of the *China Mail*, when he knighted Robert Fraser-Smith, the editor of the rival *Hongkong Telegraph*, and all his staff. Bain's campaign against him destroyed any chance he had of raising money in Hong Kong.

Two years later the King managed to raise the finance he needed in Belgium. He left Antwerp aboard a borrowed yacht to the strains of the 'Hymn of the Sedangs', his new national anthem, which was composed one evening in the Moulin Rouge in Montmartre. The tune is somewhat similar to the cancan.

On arriving in Singapore he discovered that his kingdom had been taken over by the French government. To avoid arrest he went to Malaya, where he set up a business exporting birds' nests to China. He died there from a snake bite.

A birds' nest seller

MARQUIS ANTONINE DE MORES
EMPEROR OF THE BADLANDS

The Marquis Antonine de Morès came to Hong Kong on 22 November 1888 for one reason only: to change ship. He was on his way to French Indochina, where he had plans to build a railway. The French Marquis was invited to dinner by the Governor, Sir William Des Voeux, who was a friend of his father.

Des Voeux knew nothing of the Marquis' colourful past. De Morès had married an American and tried cattle ranching in the wilds of North Dakota. He built a town called Medora and soon became known as the 'Emperor of the Badlands'. The fiery, cow-punching Marquis got involved in a cattle war with his neighbours. He was nearly lynched after bush-whacking the opposition. Drama stalked him like a tiger.

In Hong Kong the Marquis stayed at the Hong Kong Hotel, where he is supposed to have met that notorious con man Marie-Charles David de Mayréna, the King of the Sedangs. Legend has it that these two adventurers fought a duel.

The historian Henry Lethbridge, in his book *Hong Kong: Stability and Change,* has investigated this rumour and found no evidence to prove that it was true. One of his theories is that possibly the story was put about by Mayréna 'as a form of self-advertisement', in order to establish that he was a gentleman. It would seem that in those days only a gentleman would have been permitted to fight a duel with a French Marquis.

The railway project collapsed. De Morès next attempted to overthrow France's Third Republic. He created a street gang of hooligans similar to Hitler's storm-troopers in the 1930s. The main difference was that De Morès dressed his 'brownshirts' in purple blouses and cowboy hats.

After a brief spell in prison, he turned his attention to the destruction of the British Empire. Before he could accomplish his mission he was assassinated while crossing the Libyan desert. His American wife, who was convinced that the Emperor of the Badlands had been murdered by the British Secret Service, hired a posse of American cowboys to scour the Sahara for his assassins.

124

RUDYARD KIPLING
CHRONICLER OF EMPIRE

'The steamer groaned and grunted and howled because she was so damp and miserable, and I groaned also because the guide-book said Hong Kong had the finest harbour in the world, and I could not see two hundred yards in any direction.'

It was a foggy April day when Rudyard Kipling, the Apostle of the British Raj, penned these words in 1889. Later he and his friend, the Professor, dutifully took the funicular railway up to the Peak: 'We came to a meeting-place of the winds, eighteen hundred feet above all the world, and saw forty miles of clouds.'

Perhaps it was the weather that drove Kipling to seek comfort in a girlie bar: 'That the world should hold French, German and Italian ladies of the Ancient Profession is no great marvel,' he wrote, 'but it is to one who has lived in India something shocking to meet again Englishwomen in the same sisterhood.'

One of the 'sisterhood' was a lady known as 'Corinthian Kate'. Unfortunately, Kipling had told her he was a doctor and he felt that it was his duty to spend the night looking after his patient, who was 'quivering on the verge of a complaint called the "jumps"'.

'Daylight showed her purple-eyed, slack-cheeked, and staring, racked with a headache and the nervous twitches...Kate swayed to and fro and cursed God and man and earth and heaven with puffed

Rudyard Kipling

lips...and the half dozen little dogs that infested the room removed
themselves beyond the reach of Corinthian Kate's hand or foot.'

Kipling had spent thirty dollars. He was rather ashamed of himself
but, in spite of the dreadful weather and the appalling Kate, he was
very impressed by Hong Kong. 'This beats Calcutta into a hamlet,' he
wrote. 'When I die I would be a Taipan at Hong-Kong.' But he added a
bit of advice: 'When you are in the China Seas be careful to keep all
your flannel-wear to hand.'

The Peak Tramway

REVEREND JOHN ARTHUR TURNER

VICTORIAN EVANGELIST

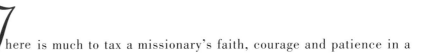

'*T*here is much to tax a missionary's faith, courage and patience in a Colony like Hong Kong,' wrote the Reverend John Arthur Turner, 'where gigantic evils stalk proudly along...'

The gigantic evils that Turner identified were gambling and drunkenness and 'certain sins fostered by the presence of a mixed population and a looser public opinion'. In 1894 the word *sex* was strictly taboo. It would not have been proper for a Wesleyan minister to use such a vile

The one-shilling stands at Happy Valley Racecourse

word in a travel book on Kwangtung province.

The Reverend Turner was a missionary based in southern China. He was impressed by the Tai Tam Reservoir, the Peak Tramway, the Alice Memorial Hospital and the numerous places of worship in the colony. He was delighted by the 'exquisitely kept cemeteries' at Happy Valley.

Unfortunately, once a year there was a race meeting, when the population of Hong Kong descended on Happy Valley: 'One would think the shades must be disturbed in their resting places by the presence of such a gay and giddy throng, where on this day of vice is allowed to flaunt itself without shame.'

The Governor of Hong Kong, Sir William Robinson, obviously agreed with him. In 1892, the year after Turner left China, Robinson banned gambling at Happy Valley. The ban lasted for two years, before the puritanical Governor caved in to public pressure and was forced to lift it.

Turner was highly critical of the British 'Tommies' and 'Bluejackets': 'They drink like fishes, ride round the town in rickshaws, making night hideous with their shouts, eat over-ripe fruit from street stalls, are stricken with cholera, and die in a few hours.'

Turner preached that 'total abstinence' was the duty of soldiers and sailors. His failure to persuade the drunken and licentious soldiery to refrain from strong drink was possibly only exceeded by his failure to convert a significant number of Chinese to Christianity.

HRH DUKE OF CONNAUGHT
SON OF QUEEN VICTORIA

Arthur, Duke of Connaught, was the third son of Queen Victoria. He visited Hong Kong twice. The first occasion was in 1890, when he was accompanied by his wife, Princess Louise Marguerite of Prussia. Among his public duties the Duke laid the foundation stone for Sir Paul Chater's grand Praya Reclamation Scheme, which covered an area of sixty-five acres between HMS *Tamar* and West Point.

Chater was something of a toady where royalty was concerned. He not only named the new road Connaught Road, after the Duke, but also commissioned a statue of His Royal Highness. There was a protracted disagreement as to where this monument should be placed. As a result, it was left to moulder in a matshed for a dozen years. It was finally unveiled in Statue Square in 1902 by Major-General Sir William Gascoigne, the Acting Governor.

In 1906, when the Duke revisited Hong Kong, it was decided to move the statue to Pedder Street, opposite Blake Pier. The *South China Morning Post* described the operation: 'A yelling horde of coolies ac-

The unveiling of the Duke of Connaught's statue in Statue Square

companied the Duke of Connaught to Blake Pier yesterday. People rushed to the windows and out of doors to investigate. It was the passing of the Duke, not in person, only in bronze. The Committee has conceived the brilliant idea of confronting the Duke on landing with his own image. It is sincerely hoped he will survive the shock.'

The Duke was on his way to Japan, to present the Emperor with the Order of the Garter. In return, the grateful Emperor awarded the Duke with the Order of Chrysanthemum. Wherever he went he was greeted by hordes of schoolchildren shouting *banzai* and 'God Save the King'. These children would have come from the same generation of Japanese who smashed his statue to smithereens during the dark days of World War Two.

The first visit of the Duke of Connaught in 1890.
A page from the Illustrated London News

The Duke's statue after its move to Pedder Street

The Duke of Connaught in a sedan chair on his second visit to the colony in 1906

The Duke and Duchess of Connaught buying furs in Japan

THE BALDWIN BROTHERS
AMERICAN AERONAUTS

The balloon went up! 'Mr Baldwin came down as gently as a bird on an unwary worm.' This is how the *Hongkong Telegraph* described the colony's first balloon ascent and parachute descent, which took place at Happy Valley on 3 January 1891.

The Baldwin Brothers were showmen as much as hot-air balloonists. To amuse the crowd, while their balloon was being inflated, the younger Baldwin flung himself off an eighty-foot bamboo tower into a net.

Before his spectacular parachute jump, young Baldwin performed gymnastics on a trapeze fifty feet below the balloon. His elder brother, incidentally, claimed to have invented the parachute.

The show was such a success that a Señor Hernandez, who liked to call himself 'Mexican Bill', tried to emulate the Baldwins' feat the next year: 'Up he went, and so did the balloon in flames, and the next the spectators knew was that a scorched and indignant señor was among them, weeping, as the whole thing burnt out,' stated one report.

Twenty years later, the Baldwins were back in town. In 1910 Mr Ivy Baldwin put on another display. It was not quite so successful. Although hundreds of people crammed into an enclosure near Holt's Wharf for the take-off, most people preferred to watch the event for free from the harbour's edge. There were no gymnastics this time. As the balloon rose over the harbour, Baldwin let off a primitive form of smoke bomb to thrill the crowd. Then he jumped: 'In a few ticks of the watch, the parachute spread like an umbrella.' With a gigantic splash, Ivy Baldwin fell like Icarus into the harbour. Unlike the mythical Greek birdman, Ivy lived to fly another day—but then Icarus was not wearing a Mae West.

The Baldwins turned up again in Hong Kong the next year with three biplanes. The government this time refused them permission to fly.

NICHOLAS
TSAREVICH OF RUSSIA

*T*he future Tsar of all Russians, the ill-fated Nicholas II, landed in Hong Kong on 4 April 1891, 'amidst the booming of guns and a feeble attempt at a British cheer'. He was greeted by the Governor, Sir William Des Voeux, and inspected a guard of honour from the Argyll and Sutherland Highlanders at Murray Pier.

The ceremonies over, Nicholas and his entourage embarked on a gigantic shopping spree. They descended on the Kelly & Walsh bookshop, where they bought up its stock of photographs of local scenery (this was before the days of picture postcards) and 'acquired several magnificent gold, ivory, and lacquer cabinets, immense bronze vases, and a few other trifles' from Kuhn's, the antique dealers. They spent thousands of dollars.

On the way to Hong Kong they had stopped off in Bangkok, where the King of Siam had presented them with two baby elephants and a number of white monkeys, as gifts for the Tsar.

Unfortunately, during the voyage the monkeys fell overboard and were drowned, while the baby elephants died of cold. Although there was no chance of finding replacement elephants in Hong Kong, monkeys were another matter. The *Hongkong Telegraph* reported: 'Escaping from the crowd of gazers, the royal lot hired ordinary street rickshaws, in which they drove, much like a group of cheap trippers, along Queen's Road West to look at Chinatown. Some of the entourage tried to find a place where a white monkey was for sale. The monkey quest being fruitless, the party returned to their ship.'

The newspaper was not particularly impressed by the twenty-three-year-old heir to the throne of Russia or his taste in civilian clothes: 'The Czarewitch was particularly inconspicuous when in mufti; he wore a second-rate sort of grey suit, very little jewelry, and, being comparatively short (besides being snub-nosed) he was quite over shadowed by his gigantic followers. He is not said to be brilliant intellectually, taking after his father in that respect.'

A Hong Kong porcelain shop

DR JOSE RIZAL
HERO OF THE PHILIPPINES

any cities of the world display commemorative plaques on their buildings to tell you where the famous once lived. In Hong Kong there are only seven such plaques, four of which commemorate Dr Sun Yat-sen, the founder of the Republic of China. Sir Kai Ho Kai, a somewhat dubious politician, also gets one. Kai Tak airport is named after him and Au Tak, his partner in the Great New Territories Land Swindle of 1898. The Scottish missionary, Dr James Legge, is also honoured.

There is a plaque to Dr José Rizal, the national hero of the Philippines, on the wall of a massive glass and marble structure at number 5 D'Aguilar Street in Central. His house stood on this site, but his first clinic was over a grog shop in Duddell Street. Unfortunately the building often shook with the sound of drunken debauchery. This was not compatible with his work—eye surgery—so he moved to D'Aguilar Street.

Rizal was known as 'The Spanish Doctor' and was a popular member of the community. He met his wife, Miss Josephine Bracken, in Hong Kong.

The Spanish colonial government in Manila did not approve of Dr Rizal. He had written a book called *Noli Me Tangere* (Do Not Touch Me), which has been unkindly described as the *Uncle Tom's Cabin* of the Philippines' revolutionary movement. It was printed in Europe and smuggled into Manila via Hong Kong.

In late 1892, Rizal was lured by false promises to the Philippines, where he was immediately arrested by the Spanish. This act of treachery raised a storm in Hong Kong. The indomitable Robert Fraser-Smith, the editor of the *Hongkong Telegraph* wrote: 'Here is a man of the highest standing, a resident of the community, a gentleman, a scholar and a patriot, decoyed from our city and sent to a sure and speedy death on a palpably trumped up charge.'

In spite of the efforts of Fraser-Smith and the British Consul in Manila, Dr Rizal was executed by a Spanish firing squad in 1896.

Portrait of Dr Jose Rizal, by Tomas Bernardo

DR SHIMBASABURO KITASATO
JAPANESE BACTERIOLOGIST

*P*eople come to Hong Kong for many very different reasons: shopping business, political freedom or the lure of the Orient. Dr Shimbasaburo Kitasato was unique. He came to the colony to study the bubonic plague, also known as the 'Black Death'. Kitasato was a Japanese bacteriologist—and a very brave one.

A terrible epidemic raged through Tai Ping Shan in 1894. Tai Ping Shan means 'peaceful hill'. It was an overcrowded, pestiferous Chinese slum. The Governor, Sir William Robinson, sent in the 'Whitewash Brigade' to clean up the infected area, demolish buildings and remove the bodies. The men of the King's Shropshire Light Infantry did most of this dangerous work. Many of them died as a result.

While thousands fled the colony, the courageous Dr Kitasato arrived and set to work tirelessly on his research. He is credited with discovering the causative organism, *yersinia pestis*, which is named after another bacteriologist who 'discovered' it a little later. Kitasato established the theory that the plague was carried by rats.

Bubonic plague victims

138

The 'Whitewash Brigade' cleaning up Tai Ping Shan

The men of the King's Shropshire Light Infantry had to do some of the most unpleasant work during the plague

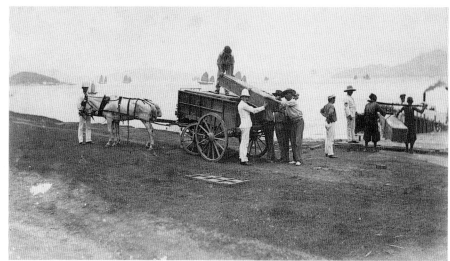

We do not know if he was awarded the Hong Kong Plague Medal, as no accurate records exist. These medals are nowadays much prized by collectors. A number of silver inkstands were also presented by the Hong Kong Government.

When the bubonic plague broke out again the new Governor, Sir Henry Blake, offered a reward of two cents, which he later increased to five cents, for every rat caught. His campaign became a spectacular success. In 1900 alone, 43,000 dead rodents were collected. Then somebody smelled a rat. Blake's enlightened policy had backfired. It was discovered that Hong Kong's ever-rapacious entrepreneurs were importing thousands of rats from China.

Faint-hearted residents and tourists will be comforted to learn that the last outbreak of the bubonic plague in Hong Kong was in 1923. This dreadful pestilence has been contained, thanks to the courageous efforts of valiant pioneers like Dr Shimbasaburo Kitasato.

EMILIO AGUINALDO Y FAMY
FILIPINO REVOLUTIONARY

*H*ong Kong was originally conceived by the British to provide a safe haven for their merchants trading in the Far East. Over the years it has provided sanctuary for millions of refugees from China, Vietnam and many other nations. Amongst them were one or two genuine revolutionaries.

The Philippines was a colony of Spain when General Emilio Aguinaldo y Famy led a rebellion against the colonial power. At the time Spain was having problems with another of its colonies, Cuba, and was unable to provide enough troops to put down Aguinaldo's insurrection. The Spanish offered to pay Aguinaldo a bribe of $1,700,000 if he stopped the fighting and agreed to go into exile.

Emilio Aguinaldo y Famy

On 27 December 1897, Aguinaldo and his junta of twenty Filipinos arrived in Hong Kong. The Spanish had deposited an advance of $400,000 in the Hongkong and Shanghai Bank under his name. Aguinaldo set up his headquarters in Peel Street, close to the Central district. One of the junta, Isabelo Artacho, threatened to sue Aguinaldo for what he considered his share of the bribe. While the junta was arguing about how to spend the money, Aguinaldo did a deal with the American Consul-General in Hong Kong, Rounceville Wildman, to buy 200,000 rifles.

He paid Wildman $50,000 for the first shipment, which was delivered, and another $67,000 for a further shipment, which did not arrive. The money vanished mysteriously—probably into the pocket of Rounceville Wildman. The Spanish government never paid Aguinaldo the rest of the money.

In 1898 war broke out between America and Spain. America had promised to recognize Filipino independence if Aguinaldo and his patriots helped them fight the Spanish. Aguinaldo agreed. Admiral Dewey sunk the Spanish fleet in Manila Bay and, on 12 June 1898, Aguinaldo declared the Philippines a republic, with himself as its first President.

However, the Americans had no intention of leaving the Philippines and it became a 'commonwealth' of the United States of America. Everybody seems to have double-crossed everybody else. Rudyard Kipling, the poet laureate of imperialism, commemorated the event by composing a poem which begins with the deathless line, 'Take up the White Man's Burden'.

LI HUNG-CHANG
CHINESE STATESMAN

Li Hung-chang played a leading part in putting down the Taiping Rebellion, fighting side-by-side with 'Chinese Gordon' and his Ever-Victorious Army. For the next forty years, whenever a crisis between imperial China and the West became a disaster, Li was given the thankless task of cleaning up somebody else's mess. His signature can be found on a dozen or so unequal treaties, including the lease on the New Territories.

The British take-over of the New Territories did not run smoothly and there was some fighting. The Governor, Sir Henry Blake, removed the gates of Kat Hing Wai walled village and sent them back to Ireland to decorate his home, Myrtle Grove. Li Hung-chang arrived in Hong Kong in June 1900. He soon sorted everything out—mainly in Britain's favour. He was known in the West as the 'Great Viceroy'.

With some justification, Li Hung-chang is not popular in China today. It has been proved that he accepted an enormous bribe from the Russians. However, his greatest crime seems to have been culinary.

Li Hung-chang

The story goes that late one night he arrived in an American city and demanded a meal in a Cantonese restaurant. All the restaurant owner could do was put together an impromptu dish made up of the day's leftovers. This Li ate with great relish. The next day the owner re-created the same dish at the request of his curious American customers. He called the concoction 'Chop Suey'.

Veterans of the Ever-Victorious Army

Sir Henry Blake's name was immortalized when the *bauhinia
blakeana*, Hong Kong's national flower, was named after him. For some
inexplicable reason China's National People's Congress has decided that
Blake's bauhinia will grace the future SAR flag. We are told that the
decisions of the Congress cannot be altered. It would seem that Hong
Kong is now doomed to have its flag, coins and banknotes decorated
with the image of a sterile hybrid named after an arch-colonial Irish
vandal.

PRINCE CHUN
MANCHU PRINCE

Prince Chun, brother of the reigning Emperor of China, arrived in Hong Kong aboard the German ship *Bayern* on 25 July 1901. He was on his way to Germany to apologize to the Kaiser for the murder of the German Minister in Peking, Baron Von Ketteler, who was killed during the Boxer Rebellion the previous year.

At Blake Pier he was met by a number of British officials, including Reginald Johnston. Because of the sensitive nature of his mission, the Prince preferred that he did not receive a ceremonial welcome. There

Prince Chun's visit to the B & S dock

Blake

Blake Pier

were to be no salutes from the warships in the harbour and no military parade.

Johnston described how 'four red-coated chair-bearers bore him swiftly from the water-front'. The *Hongkong Weekly Press*, however, presented a very different picture: 'As matters turned out the police escort was not visible until an absurdly late hour in the proceedings, and our visitors had to force their way through a gaping and unmannerly crowd up to Government House.'

Hongkong.

The police guard-of-honour may have been late, but fortunately the crowds were very small, unlike Prince Chun's previous stopover in Shanghai, where thousands had turned out to greet him.

After admiring the portrait of Queen Victoria at Government House, the Prince went to the Chinese Club. He then took the Peak Tram and had tea with the Governor, Sir Henry Blake, on the Peak. Afterwards, he returned to the *Bayern* and the tender care of Major-General Von Richter and the 9th Company, 4th Ostasiatische Battalion of German Infantry.

147

Prince Chun's German escort also included a company of dog-handlers called 'Jagers'. They entertained the Prince on his long voyage to Genoa with endless canine demonstrations. Primarily, these dogs had been trained to sniff out dead and wounded soldiers on the field of battle.

Prince Chun later became Regent to the Emperor of China. His son, Pu Yi, was the famous 'Last Emperor'. Sir Reginald Johnston was his English tutor; and he looked nothing like Peter O'Toole.

Prince Chun, when Regent of China, with his two sons,
Pu Chieh and Pu Yi, the 'Last Emperor'

SIR MILES LAMPSON
BRITISH DIPLOMAT

Miles Lampson was Acting Secretary to the Duke of Connaught during his mission to Japan to deliver the Order of the Garter from King Edward VII to the Emperor. The mission stopped off in Hong Kong on the way, in February 1906. Lampson kept a diary during the trip.

The day after they landed, the royal party went by steamer to the Golf Club in Deep Water Bay for lunch. They attempted to walk back to Government House, although sedan chairs had been provided: 'When one got blown one got into one's chair, and the wretched coolies had to drag me up the hill.'

Lampson was most impressed by the chair coolies, 'magnificent fellows, with calves such as I never saw before'. The Duke, because of his rank, was carried by twenty men, whereas 'more humble individuals'

A Hong Kong sedan chair

Mountain chairs and rickshaws

like Lampson only had four. This was a bit unfair as Lampson was an enormous man.

The first dinner that evening was a Chinese banquet of around thirty different exotic dishes, including stewed lichen, birds' nest in syrup and sharks' fins. 'The food was mostly insipid to a degree, and in some cases positively nasty,' Lampson wrote in his diary. An hour later they had 'a large and most excellent supper' at the Hong Kong Club.

Lampson's dislike for Chinese cuisine was exceeded only by his hatred for strong drink. Many years later, when he was British Minister in China, he was notorious for his 'fulminations against Consular drunkenness'.

During World War Two he was British Ambassador in Cairo, where he achieved immortality by having a verse devoted to him and his unfortunate wife in 'The Ballad of King Farouk and Queen Farida'. It begins:

> 'Oh it's not hard to see poor Delilah's up a tree,
> For "she" wears the horns in the Lampson family.
> Old Sir Miles with his wiles
> In advance tries to...'

The rest of the verse is too obscene to print in this book.

150

CHARLES VAN DEN BORN

BELGIAN AVIATOR

A number of American and French aviators wanted to stage Hong Kong's first powered flight, but they were refused permission by the Hong Kong Government on the grounds that they were a security risk. The official line was: 'Government, however well disposed towards the airmen, cannot allow promiscuous flying about the Island and the Territory.'

The authorities finally relented and allowed Charles Van Den Born, a Belgian pilot, to attempt a flight at Shatin. Why a Belgian should be considered any more trustworthy than a Frenchman or an American is not clear. On 18 March 1911, the Governor, Sir Frederick Lugard, and thousands of spectators went to Shatin on a special train to witness the Colony's first flight. The cost of tickets ranged from fifty cents to three dollars, with a plane ride costing as much as seventy-five bucks.

Unfortunately, there was a strong wind and Van Den Born's Farman biplane could not take off. Most of the disappointed spectators caught the 5.10 pm train back to Kowloon. After the Governor and the multitudes had departed, the wind dropped and Charles Van Den Born took to the

Charles Van Den Born

Van Den Born's biplane at Shatin

151

skies, watched only by a few despondent water buffaloes and a handful of decrepit Hakka peasants.

A week later there was another demonstration at Shatin. Those aviation buffs who went along witnessed Hong Kong's first plane crash. With a sickening thud, Van Den Born's machine bit the dust while trying to avoid a crowd of schoolboys from Queen's College, who were playing on the landing strip.

The 'Winged Walloon' was unhurt and lived to fly another day. He moved on to Canton where he put on a flying show for the Manchu General, Fu Chi, known as the 'Guardian of the Cantonese'. Unfortunately, just after the show a republican gunman shot General Fu dead. Further aviation displays in China were cancelled.

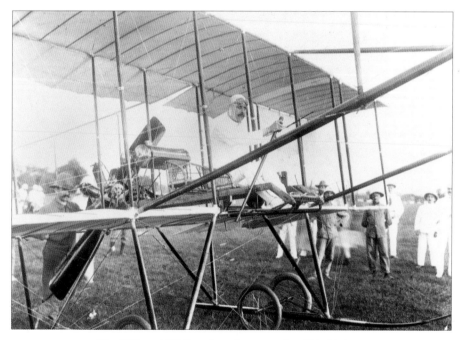

The 'Winged Walloon' at the controls of his biplane

Van Den Born's 'Farman' at Shatin

The first powered flight in Hong Kong, 18 March 1911

A Hakka boy with a water buffalo

The 'Farman II' biplane

'VINEGAR JOE' STILWELL
AMERICAN GENERAL

In November 1911, the young Lieutenant Joseph Stilwell of the United States Army visited Hong Kong. Six weeks earlier China had erupted in revolution against the Ching dynasty. There was chaos in the Middle Kingdom. Stilwell wrote at the time: 'All the trouble was worked up by the bloody British who are trying to make things as bad as possible to justify intervention on their part.'

In later life, 'Vinegar Joe' was well known for his Anglophobia, but to blame the British for starting the 1911 Revolution was perhaps a little extreme—even for him.

To be fair, Vinegar Joe was not totally critical of everything he saw in Hong Kong. He loved the view from the top of the Peak. He was fascinated by the new haircuts of those Hong Kong Chinese who had recently cut off their *queues* as a symbolic gesture in support of the revolution. He was very impressed by the British drill sergeants, but he thought that their officers were 'untidy, grouchy, sloppy, fooling around with canes, a bad example for the men'.

During World War Two, General Stilwell was Deputy Supreme Commander of the Allied Forces in Southeast Asia. Unfortunately, the Supreme Commander was Lord Louis Mountbatten, who was not only English, but also minor royalty. As well as disliking the

General Joseph Stilwell

British, Stilwell was a staunch republican, but Mountbatten got off lightly in comparison with Chiang Kai-shek.

It was the Nationalist leader who was the main target of his 'black bile and excoriating tongue'. Stilwell was Chiang's Chief of Staff and hated him and loathed the ruling Kuomintang. 'A one-party government supported by a Gestapo and headed by an unbalanced man with little education.' His nickname for the Generalissimo was the 'Peanut'.

Stilwell was undoubtedly a fine general, but most of his military triumphs are long forgotten. Instead he is remembered as Vinegar Joe—America's monumental public relations disaster.

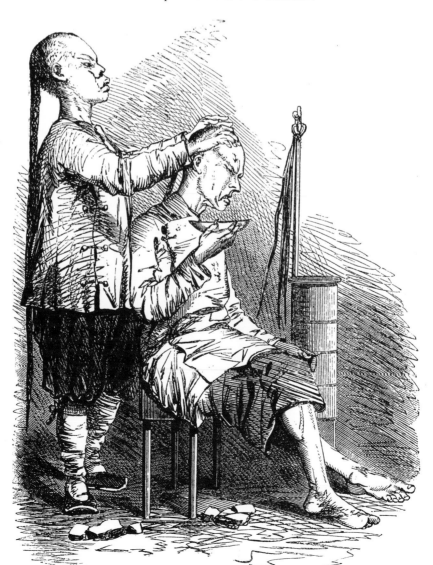

Caricature of a Chinese barber

EDWARD
PRINCE OF WALES
HEIR APPARENT

By the time the Prince of Wales arrived in Hong Kong on 6 April 1922, he had been touring the British Empire for half a year. He had shaken hands with thousands of his future subjects, listened to hundreds of boring speeches, attended dozens of banquets and ploughed through mounds of strange, rich, indigestible food. He had shot tigers in Nepal, gone pig-sticking at Jodhpur and come a close second in a sack race in Malta.

When he reached Hong Kong he was probably feeling rather jaded. The weather was awful. The magnificent decorations on the Peak were shrouded in fog. He met hundreds of school children, boy scouts and girl guides, inspected the 102nd Grenadiers (Indian Army), received an honorary degree from the university and an address from the Masons. He played polo, went to the races, did some shopping in Kowloon and insulted the Governor, Sir Reginald Stubbs, by behaving badly at a Government House dinner given in his honour. It was a lot to cram into two days.

His Royal Highness also upset Executive Councillor, Sir Paul Chater, an indefatigable royalist, who had raised $50,000 for a statue of the Prince. Edward did not warm to the idea of having his statue join the graven images of Queen Victoria, King Edward VII, Queen Alexandra, King George V, Queen Mary, a bank manager, two lions and an Irish governor—all of which already decorated Statue Square. It was a depressing thought.

He suggested instead 'that some very good thing be done for the community of Hong Kong in his name' with the money. After careful consideration as to what would best benefit the community as a whole, the $50,000 was given to the British Legion.

On the death of his father, King George V, in 1936, Prince Edward became King Edward VIII; but he abdicated in order to marry Mrs Wallis Simpson, an American divorcee. Today, he is remembered as the Duke of Windsor.

Prince of Wales taking tea at the Pavilion, Hong Kong

Inspecting the Guard of Honour

A section of the Chinese procession

Prince of Wales in the uniform of the 35/36 Jacob's Horse

DR SUN YAT-SEN
PRESIDENT OF CHINA

When Dr Sun Yat-sen, founder of the Republic of China and its first President, returned to Canton in triumph in 1923, he stopped off in Hong Kong. He received an enthusiastic welcome. Dr Sun had studied medicine in Hong Kong when he was a young man. On his return, he was invited to speak at his old university.

Dr Sun described the University of Hong Kong as his intellectual birthplace. He explained that when he returned home during vacations he was horrified by the corruption in China. There was disorder instead of order, insecurity instead of security. There was laughter when he explained that he even had to be his own policeman and had had to see that his rifle was in order. He explained that Hsiang-shan, where he lived, and Hong Kong, were only fifty miles apart. He said that he got his revolutionary ideas entirely in Hong Kong.

Dr Sun told his audience how his organization overthrew the Ching Dynasty twelve years earlier and established a republic. He explained that they had not succeeded very well with their republican form of government yet, because the movement had not run its full course.

His final statement expressed sentiments one would not have expected from the founder of the Chinese Republic: 'My fellow students; you and I have studied in this English colony and in an English University and we must learn by English examples. We must carry this English example of good government to China.'

As well as running Dr Sun's speech, the *Hongkong Telegraph* of that day carried a front page story of a six million dollar British loan to Dr Sun. It claimed that the money would only be available if Dr Sun agreed to abandon Bolshevism and sever all his connections with the labour unions. There was speculation among cynics that Dr Sun's splendid pro-British speech and the six million dollar loan were not entirely unconnected.

Photo Taber, San Francisco.

仙逸孫

Dr Sun Yat-sen

*University of
Hong Kong*

'TWO-GUN' COHEN
SOLDIER OF FORTUNE

*Y*ears before Dr Sun Yat-sen became President of China, he had hired Morris Abraham Cohen as a bodyguard during a tour of Canada. A few years later, when Dr Sun passed through Hong Kong in 1923 on his way from Shanghai to Canton, he had just re-hired Cohen.

When Dr Sun visited Government House, he put Colonel 'Two-Gun' Cohen in charge of his security. It was Cohen's first major operation of this sort. Confidently he posted his guards around the front gate. He was rather pleased with himself until the Governor, Sir Reginald Stubbs, sent his aide-de-camp to have a word with him.

Movietone News cameraman Marvin Farkas filming 'Two-Gun' Cohen

*Marvin Farkas being
arrested for filming
'Two-Gun' Cohen*

The ADC tactfully pointed out that, while the main gates were well guarded, there were five other back gates that had no security at all. Assassins don't usually use the front door. 'I don't suppose they'll be wanting to write their names in the Governor's book,' remarked the ADC dryly. 'Be a sport and show me what to do!' replied Cohen.

On their departure, the Governor thanked Cohen for the splendid job he had done. The lordly ADC, who was standing behind the Governor, winked at Cohen. 'If the Statue of Liberty in New York harbour had looked down and winked, I couldn't have been more surprised and I just winked back—a sort of reflex action—but the Governor never moved a muscle on his face.'

After that Dr Sun had the best security in the world. He died in 1925, but 'Two-Gun' Cohen stayed on in China. He was made a general in the Chinese army. Only two other British soldiers ever made that rank—'Chinese Gordon' and Frank 'One-Arm' Sutton.

The lad from the East End of London was also probably the only European member of the Tsing Chung-Hui Triad Society, an organisation which he joined while a real estate salesman in Edmonton, Canada, years before he met Dr Sun.

TREBITSCH LINCOLN
SCOUNDREL

A stocky little man with Kaiser Bill moustaches landed in Hong Kong in September 1927. He was immediately detained by the police. His passport identified him as H Ruh. However, he was known to the police as Trebitsch Lincoln: missionary, journalist, politician, oil baron, spy, revolutionary, con man, holy man, beggarman, thief.

Born in Budapest, he stole his first gold watch at the age of eighteen and left home in a hurry. His first real job was as an Anglican missionary, in Montreal, converting Jews to Christianity. Lincoln took British nationality and in 1910 he became the Member of Parliament for Darlington. His parliamentary career lasted for less than a year.

Lincoln then went into the oil business. Having committed a massive fraud, he fled to the United States, where he was arrested. While in police custody in New York in the middle of World War One, he unwisely published his famous book, *Revelations of an International Spy*. He was deported to Britain, where he spent three years in jail. He was lucky not to have been shot. He then went to Germany, where he attempted to overthrow the Weimar Republic. The Kapp Putsch failed and he fled to China, where he became a gun-runner.

Abbot CHAO KUNG

POPPE ROAD
FU SHAN LI 6/8
Third Special Area

TIENTSIN

China

照空大和尚　收啓

禰善里八號

七緯路

天津特別三區

*Trebitsch Lincoln's
visiting card*

He explained to the Hong Kong Police that he was trying to get to India, Burma or Ceylon in order to study Buddhism. However, Lincoln was banned from all British territories worldwide. 'I could easily have forged a passport,' he explained to the police, 'but all this lying is against the principles of Buddhism.' The British put him on the first boat to China clutching his H Ruh passport. It was, of course, a forgery.

Lincoln actually became a Buddhist monk. Posing as the Venerable Abbot Chao Kung he went on a recruiting campaign to Europe. He brought back a dozen rich converts to his Buddhist House in Shanghai. The abbot spent most of the 1930s publishing books on Buddhism and fleecing his converts. He died in 1943.

Trebitsch Lincoln in the guise of the Venerable Abbot Chao Kung

165

BENGAL
THE WONDER PONY

engal the 'Wonder Pony' was owned for many years by the notorious gun-runner Frank 'One-Arm' Sutton. Bengal was a racehorse. Frank Sutton had lost an arm fighting in Gallipoli in World War One. He spent his time in hospital designing the Sutton Mortar, a lethal little weapon that was cheap and relatively easy to manufacture.

Sutton made thousands of these small mortars at the Mukden Arsenal for the 'Old Marshal' Chang Tso-lin, the Manchurian warlord. Then, in 1924, Sutton led an attack on the Great Wall of China. He had little difficulty in capturing it because the enemy had left a gate open. As a reward for this triumph, the Old Marshal promoted Sutton to the rank of general.

It was to be Sutton's lucky year. He won $224,000 on a Shanghai sweepstake and bought Bengal the Wonder Pony from David Fraser, the Reuter's correspondent in Peking.

Before World War Two, only Mongolian ponies were raced in Hong Kong and the other treaty ports. Bengal beat almost everything that moved in northern China. Out of forty-two starts he had forty-one wins. The same jockey, Roy Davis, rode him in every race.

The Wonder Pony never raced in Shanghai, where Sir Victor Sassoon completely dominated the racing scene. Sir Victor's favourite saying was, 'There is only one race greater than the Jews and that is the Derby'. He was fabulously rich, and became the leading owner simply by buying any horse that beat one from his stable.

One-Arm Sutton sold Bengal in 1928 to a mysterious Hong Kong buyer. Everybody assumed that the new owner was Sir Victor. They were

Racing at Happy Valley

quite right, of course. Bengal won his first race at Happy Valley, the Great Southern Stakes, in 1928, but in his second race he came in a miserable third. The Wonder Pony unfortunately had hoof trouble. Sir Victor never raced him again.

Hong Kong was not an auspicious place for either the Wonder Pony or his master. No one knows the fate of Bengal; but Sutton died in Stanley Concentration Camp in 1944.

The Great Wall of China

'One-Arm' Sutton's visiting card

MAJOR GENERAL F. A. SUTTON,

MANAGING DIRECTOR,
F. A. SUTTON, LTD.   2ND. FLOOR, SHELL HOUSE
HONG KONG   PHONE 25435

SIR NOEL COWARD

PLAYWRIGHT

*I*t is fortunate for Hong Kong's tourist industry that the playwright, Sir Noel Coward, visited Hong Kong in 1929. It was the same year in which he wrote his famous song *Mad Dogs and Englishmen*, which contains the immortal lines:

> 'In Hong Kong
> They strike a gong
> And fire off a noondaygun
> To reprimand each inmate
> Who's in late.'

Coward got it wrong. The purpose of firing the noondaygun was to let people know when it was midday. In the Victorian era watches were a luxury.

He probably got the custom muddled up with Quebec in Canada, where they fire both a noondaygun and an evening gun, the original purpose being to alert soldiers to the fact that it was time for them to return to their barracks, where they would be 'reprimanded' if they were 'in late'. As 'Quebec' does not rhyme with 'gong', but only with 'rebec' (an obscure medieval three-stringed musical instrument) and 'xebec' (a three-masted Mediterranean vessel), we must allow him some poetic licence.

Sir Noel Coward

Sir Noel Coward firing the noondaygun

The legend behind the noondaygun is that it was fired every day at noon as a penalty for a breach of protocol caused by the firing of an illegal 21-gun salute in the 1860s. This was done by some 'grovelling sycophant' to herald the arrival of the taipan of Jardine, Matheson & Company, the head of the leading trading house known as the 'Princely Hong'.

Coward wrote his famous play *Private Lives* whilst in bed with the flu in Shanghai's Cathay Hotel, now renamed the Peace Hotel. It is not an easy play to perform. 'I've seen it massacred many times,' he said. 'An amateur group in Hong Kong decided that it was the play to do. Only four characters. Two sets. It was really terrible. Poor blind fools.'

On 20 March 1968, Sir Noel was in Hong Kong on holiday and was invited to fire the gun. He was delighted. When he arrived at Jardine's East Point godown he was late. Consequently so was the noondaygun, which boomed out three minutes after midday.

HO CHI MINH
VIETNAMESE REVOLUTIONARY

*I*n the last hundred years millions of refugees have fled to Hong Kong, including the founders of three Asian republics: Dr Sun Yat-sen, Emilio Aguinaldo and Ho Chi Minh.

Dr Sun and Aguinaldo lived openly under their own names, but Ho Chi Minh used the pseudonym Nguyen Ai Quoc—'Nguyen the Patriot'— when hiding out in darkest Kowloon City with his girlfriend, Li Sam. He did not call himself Ho Chi Minh—'He Who Enlightens'—until the early 1940s.

His presence was discovered after Shanghai Special Branch arrested the spymaster Hilaire Noulens, the head of Comintern Far Eastern Bureau. At the time Noulens controlled the famous Communist spy Richard Sorge as well as Ho Chi Minh, who was in charge of the Comintern Southern Bureau.

At the instigation of the French, Ho Chi Minh was arrested on 6 June 1931 by the Hong Kong Police. The French regarded him as a dangerous revolutionary and put pressure on the British to deport him to French Indochina, where he would certainly have been executed. His case was taken up by International Red Help, a Soviet front organization. For over eighteen months he fought extradition, aided by the British lawyer-politician, Sir Stafford Cripps.

Kowloon City

In spite of having Sir Stafford as his attorney, Ho Chi Minh won his case when it came before the Privy Council and he was smuggled out of the colony on the night of 26 January 1933. Sir Stafford, who later

became Chancellor of the Exchequer in the Attlee government of 1945, was known for his prodigious intellect. 'He has a great mind, until he makes it up,' wrote Margot Asquith.

While Sir Stafford was busy destroying the British economy, Ho Chi Minh was building the Vietnamese nation. The French, who had demanded the revolutionary's arrest and extradition, refused to pay the costs of the court case. It was left to the poor old Hong Kong taxpayer to foot the bill.

A view across paddy fields from the walls of Kowloon City

Inside Kowloon City

The entrance to Kowloon City

HENRY CHAMPLY
FRENCH WRITER

*I*t is a little unfair to call Henry Champly a pornographer. Champly saw himself as a crusading journalist whose sacred duty it was to expose the 'white slave trade' in Asia. He spent a few weeks in Hong Kong in 1932, trying to find out if any French girls were working as prostitutes in the Colony. He published his findings in a book called *The Road to Shanghai* in 1934.

He must have had good connections, because he was invited to Government House. While taking tea on the lawn, he discussed the problems of prostitution in Hong Kong with a 'Mrs X' and a British colonel.

In a chapter headed 'Is Flower Street Really Deflowered?' he describes his forlorn attempt to find a French prostitute to interview in Hong Kong's 'China Town'. He hired a leprous pimp with 'deliquescent bones, sunken eyes, and grapeous glands' to help him in his quest. As pimps go, the leper was a disaster. All he could produce was a young English girl with red hair cut in the fashion of Joan of Arc. This enraged Champly. He saw the offending hairstyle as a deliberate plot by the filthy British to sully the honour of France.

For months Champly toured Southeast Asia, China and Japan, enthusiastically interviewing dozens of perverts, pimps, paederasts and prostitutes with colourful names like Michel Scarface, the Siberian Sphinx, Nono the Tattooed and the Satanic Olga Ho Hing. On almost every page he took the trouble to point out that he was a serious journalist and how his chastity remained intact throughout his travels.

Champly's crusade to protect the virtue of French women had about as much chance of succeeding as the campaign by the *Académie Française* has of keeping the French language from being adulterated with foreign words.

Lyndhurst Terrace, Hong Kong's red light district in the 1930s

Naughty French postcards of naughty French ladies!

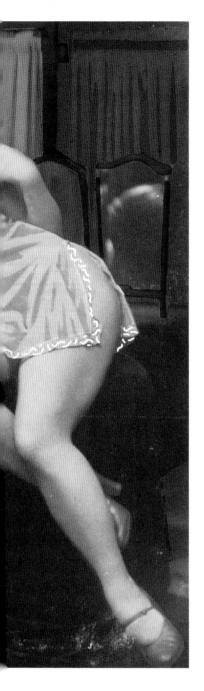

HENDRIK DE LEEUW
HACK WRITER

In the early 1930s, the 'white slave trade' was considered to be a world problem. The League of Nations sent Commissions of Enquiry all over South America and the Far East collecting data for their reports. Wherever they went, they were followed by a pack of unscrupulous journalists and hack writers who churned out endless 'serious studies' on the oldest profession. One such writer was Hendrik de Leeuw. His grand tour included Yokohama, Macau, Shanghai, Singapore, Port Said and, of course, Hong Kong.

Like Henry Champly, most of these reporters went to great lengths to explain that they were as pure as driven snow and to describe the complicated manoeuvres that they went through in order to protect their chastity. De Leeuw even went as far as to use the pseudonym of 'Mr Smith' when conducting interviews.

'I was flying under false colours, in a way, taking notes in a house of pleasure.' This is how de Leeuw describes his in-depth research study on Hong

Miss Ling, a 'sing-song girl'

178

Kong's 'Purple Mansions', which led him to the 'Club of Ducks and Mandarins' in the 'Street of Willows'.

Here he was taught international sign language that was used in the brothels of the East. He passes on a few useful tips to his readers: 'If the prostitute satisfies the prospective patron by her appearance and behaviour, he expresses his satisfaction by rubbing his forefinger under his nose.'

'Mr Smith' managed to escape with his purity intact by the simple device of scratching his right ear vigorously. Sometimes his hypocrisy knows no bounds. He wrote: 'If the only reward that I should reap would be the enlightenment of the masses, I shall indeed feel well compensated for my work.'

De Leeuw claimed that his book *Cities of Sin*, published in 1934, was a serious, in-depth exposé of the 'the huge white slave Octopus, that extends its slimy tentacles around the globe'. In fact, it is nothing more than a second-rate dirty book.

Miss Wong, a 'sing-song girl'

GEORGE BERNARD SHAW
IRISH PLAYWRIGHT

'**H**ong Kong is a damnable place!' George Bernard Shaw told reporters when he visited the colony in 1933. When asked about the Great Wall of China he replied, 'We have a much nicer wall between England and Scotland. What is a Great Wall for?'

'I don't like travel,' he added. 'Nobody likes travelling except foolish people. But women like travelling.'

He advised all the students at the University of Hong Kong to become Communists: 'If you are a revolutionary at the age of twenty, you have some chance of being up-to-date when you are forty.'

His lecture outraged the *Hongkong Telegraph* : 'When Bernard Shaw tells young students to steep themselves in revolutionary books and go up to their necks in Communism and everything of that kind, we must presume that he means precisely what he says. The street orator who used language like that would in all probability be clapped into gaol for his indiscretion.'

However, a letter published in the *South China Morning Post* took a more sensible view: 'Few people in Great Britain take Shaw's social and political views seriously and it is unfortunate that any of the British in Hong Kong should have done so. It is difficult to understand how anyone with a sense of humour could take Shaw seriously; and those without any sense of humour should have little count in our community.'

Things were somewhat different

George Bernard Shaw

The Hongkong Sunday Herald,
19 February 1933

George Bernard Shaw and his wife
with Sir Robert Hotung

back in Shaw's native Ireland. On the same page it was reported that
the County Wexford Bee Keepers' Association, of which GBS was a life
member, had just passed a resolution: 'That the name of Mr George
Bernard Shaw be removed from the list of members of the Association
in consequence of Mr Shaw's blasphemous statements concerning Christ
and Apostles in his recent book, *Adventures of a Black Girl in search
of God.*'

'Put an Irishman on the spit,' Shaw once wrote, 'and you can always
get another Irishman to turn him.'

CHARLIE CHAPLIN
FILM LEGEND

It was one of those depressing March days when, according to newspaper reports, a quarter of a million square miles of cold, dense, damp Siberian fog was drifting slowly across the South China Sea. It was so thick in Victoria Harbour that the Star Ferries were going around in circles. The liner *SS President Coolidge*, with Charlie Chaplin aboard, docked eleven hours late.

After signing a few autographs, Charlie headed for The Peninsula, where he held a press conference. His new film, *Modern Times*, had just been released and the female star, Paulette Goddard, and her mother were travelling with his party. It was rumoured that Charlie and Paulette were engaged; the news hawks were out in force.

Charlie answered the usual 'brilliantly original' questions reporters come up with on these occasions. Asked if he wanted to play Shakespeare, he remarked: 'That's a tradition that hovers around comedians.' On his personal life he was even less forthcoming: 'That's a little part of my life I like to keep to myself.'

When questioned about his trip he explained: 'I found I had three months to spare and that it would be nice to get into warm weather after going through an American winter, and we came away.' He added bitterly: 'I never thought it would be as cold as this in Hong Kong.'

Charlie Chaplin's visit was a big event in the 1930s. It is still written about, even today. But what did he actually do in Hong Kong in March 1936? The answer seems to be: nothing!

The *Hongkong Telegraph* reported that he 'intended to cram as much sight-seeing as possible into yesterday. But Friday the 13th was unlucky and he remained instead in his suite'. Charlie's party left the next morning on the *Suwa Maru* for Bali. He spent only one full day in Hong Kong. Even clowns don't go sight-seeing in the fog on a black Friday.

The Peninsula hotel in Chaplin's day

W H AUDEN
POET

*I*ts leading characters are wise and witty,
  Their suits well-tailored, and they wear them well,
  Have many a polished parable to tell
  About the *mores* of a trading city.'

This was how the British poet, W H Auden, began his sonnet *Hong Kong*. He stopped off in the colony in February 1938 with his friend, Christopher Isherwood. They were on the way to China to write a book. The meat of *Journey to a War*, the story of their travels, was written by Isherwood. It was sandwiched between two delicate slices of Auden's verse.

Isherwood was the author of the novel *Goodbye to Berlin*, on which the film *Cabaret* was based. Conscious of not being a 'real' journalist, he dressed up for the part in new boots, a turtleneck sweater and a beret. Neither Auden nor Isherwood had ever been East of Suez before.

In China they met all the right people: Chiang Kai-shek, Chou En-lai and 'Big Ears' Tu, the Shanghai gangster and mass-murderer, who was at that time running China's Red Cross. Tu politely thanked them 'in the name of humanity' for the interest they showed in the Red Cross, but Isherwood was far more interested in the man's shoes: 'Peculiarly and inexplicably terrifying were his feet, in their silk socks and smart pointed European boots, emerging from beneath the long silk gown.'

It is almost impossible for a poet to write to order, but Auden's sonnets still contain some marvellous phrases. His poem on a dead Chinese soldier begins with the dynamic line: 'Abandoned by his general and his lice.'

When the sonnet appeared in the *Ta Kung Pao* newspaper in China in April 1938, this line was tactfully changed to: 'The rich and poor are combining to fight'. Poetry tends to lose a lot in translation.

Isherwood and Auden at the start of their journey

The cover of the book by Auden and Isherwood about their trip

MADAME CHIANG KAI-SHEK
A SOONG SISTER

In February 1940, the youngest of the Soong sisters, Madame Chiang Kai-shek, visited Hong Kong for 'health reasons' and stayed with her eldest sister, Kung Ai-ling, who was reported to be the richest woman in China.

Generalissimo and Madame Chiang Kai-shek, 1948

The sisters did not get on with Ching-ling, the second sister, who was the widow of Dr Sun Yat-sen, the first President of China. After Dr Sun's death, Chiang Kai-shek, who became leader of the Kuomintang, had proposed marriage to her. Madame Sun refused his advances.

The determined Chiang married her younger sister, Mei-ling, instead. By a political marriage into the powerful Soong family, Chiang Kai-shek hoped to establish himself as the credible successor to the great Dr Sun. This infuriated Madame Sun. Chiang's policies were fundamentally opposed to those of her late husband and she would have nothing to do with him.

Madame Sun was living in Hong Kong running the 'China Defence League'. The enmity between the sisters was notorious and no one expected them to meet during Madame Chiang Kai-shek's visit. Then to everybody's surprise, the three sisters went out to dinner together at the Hong Kong Hotel.

The American writer, Emily Hahn, described how 'the dance floor looked something like the crowd at Wimbledon as couples danced past the long table, their necks turning as hard as British courtesy allowed...'

The three sisters ate their dinner, pretending to be blissfully unaware of the sensation they were causing. They had decided to sink their political differences, in order to be seen to support the United Front of the Nationalists and the Communists against the Japanese occupation of China. The dinner was the first symbolic gesture.

In December 1941, when the Japanese attacked Hong Kong, 'Two-

The Hong Kong Hotel postcard 'Chrysanthemums' is much prized by collectors

Gun' Cohen, Sun Yat-sen's former bodyguard, had great difficulty in persuading Madam Sun to escape from the colony, but he did manage to put her on the last plane from Kai Tak. She later became Honorary President of the People's Republic of China.

The Hong Kong Hotel

188

AGNES SMEDLEY
AMERICAN JOURNALIST

'Grim, sour and passionate' is how Christopher Isherwood described the American Communist journalist, Agnes Smedley. 'She is not unlike Bismarck with her close-cropped grey hair, masculine jaw, deeply-lined cheeks and bulging, luminous eyes.'

Smedley was arrested when she arrived in Hong Kong on 26 August

Agnes Smedley

1940. It was not her Communist connections which seemed to worry Special Branch, but a tempestuous affair she had conducted twenty years earlier with an Indian anarchist.

She blithely confessed that she had slept with a large number of men and added venomously that she couldn't remember if one of them had been English. 'He made so little impact on me.' She had come to Hong Kong for medical treatment and was admitted to Queen Mary Hospital, where she had an operation on her gall bladder.

The British let her stay in Hong Kong, provided that she did not indulge in political activity. It was a forlorn hope. While still in hospital, she wrote a series of scathing articles for the *South China Morning Post* attacking the social conditions in the Colony.

Shanghai Special Branch had her listed as a Soviet agent as early as 1933 and her connections with the Chinese Communists were well known. She was a friend of Chou En-lai.

It was not until after World War Two that it was discovered that she had helped the Russian Spy Master, Richard Sorge, set up his spy ring. She had recruited the Japanese journalist, Ozaki Hotsumi, his top agent. Sorge regarded her rather highly. 'She was like a man', he confessed.

In World War Two, Smedley acted as an adviser to General Stilwell and persuaded 'Vinegar Joe' to provide American arms for the Chinese Communists. After the war, she returned to America, where she was summoned to appear before the Un-American Activities Committee. She fled to England, where she died in 1950. In her will she left her ashes to Marshal Chu Teh of the People's Liberation Army.

SEICHI FUJIMURA
JAPANESE RAILWAYMAN

Seichi Fujimura was working as an engineer for the South Manchurian Railway Company when, in late 1942, he was summoned to Hong Kong by the first Japanese Governor, Lieutenant-General Rensuke Isogai, during the occupation of the Colony in World War Two. His mission was to build a new Government House.

The old Government House was falling down; prestige demanded that something should be done about it. The original neo-classical building, designed by the Surveyor-General, Charles St George Cleverly, in 1850, had been added to over the years, but Isogai wanted something more oriental. 'I would have liked to build a modern Government House,' said Fujimura, 'but Isogai and the government officials wanted to incorporate traditional Japanese architecture.'

The popular myth that the new house was cunningly constructed by British prisoners of war so that it would collapse on the head of the Japanese governor is unfortunately untrue. Not only did Fujimura design the building, but he was also responsible for the interior decorations, which included a stuffed tiger. This unlucky creature, shot at Stanley

192

*Fujimura's first design
for Government House*

in 1942, was skinned by Mr Bradbury of the Dairy Farm Company and its flesh devoured with relish by the ravenous 'gourmets' of the Hong Kong Race Club.

Unlike Hong Kong's post-war British governors, General Isogai never took up residence in Government House. Perhaps the thought of living in a building that looked like a Japanese railway station was beneath his dignity.

There has always been a trend for engineers to design Hong Kong's buildings. For many years Murray Barracks, the work of Major Aldrich of the Royal Engineers, was an ornament to the Central district. It was so much admired that, when it was demolished in 1982, its stones were numbered and put into cold storage, awaiting the opportunity to re-erect it at Stanley. Whether the headless ghost which haunted the first floor would then resurrect itself is uncertain. Perhaps in a hundred years' time the same fate will befall Sir Norman Foster's onshore-offshore oil rig, the highly acclaimed headquarters of the Hongkong and Shanghai Bank.

Government House,
with the Hongkong and Shanghai Bank in the background

194

'HIRAM' WYNNE-POTTS
ROYAL MARINE COMMANDO

Captain John Wynne-Potts, of 42 Royal Marine Commando, arrived in Hong Kong in 1945, when it was liberated after World War Two.

Wynne-Potts was known to his friends as 'Hiram'. He acquired this strange nickname a year earlier, during a series of daring buccaneering raids on the Burma coast. The commandos were supplied with American rations, among which was a brand of tinned sausages that were manufactured by Hiram J Potts. 'I liked them so much the other chaps began calling me Hiram,' Wynne-Potts explained, many years later, in an interview with the *South China Morning Post*.

As well as fighting through the Burma campaign, he saw service against EOKA terrorists in Cyprus and fought Chin Peng's Communists in the 'War of the Running Dogs' in Malaya. In all, he spent thirty-six years in the Royal Marines until his retirement in 1978.

Soon after he arrived in Hong Kong, Wynne-Potts was posted to Sai Kung, which in those days was a tiny little fishing village. Apart from a precarious goat path, the only

Inspector Wynne-Potts of the Royal Hong Kong Police examines the memorial stone on the road his father built

way you could get to the place was by sea.
So Wynne-Potts, whose only previous engi-
neering experience had been digging slit
trenches in Poona and gun emplacements in
the Orkneys, was given the job of building
a road leading to the village.

Aided by eighty marines and gangs of
Japanese and Korean prisoners-of-war, he
set to work blasting and hacking his way
through the hills. During construction, a
fellow officer who visited the site put up a
small notice which read 'Hiram's Highway'.

When the road was finished, this notice
was replaced with a massive block of
concrete, which was unveiled by the then
Commander of the British Forces, Major-
General F W Festing, and was proudly
inscribed with the deathless words 'Hiram's
Highway'.

There is no shortage of streets with
strange names in Hong Kong, but Hiram's
Highway is the only one to be named,
indirectly, after a defunct brand of tinned
American sausages.

Dai Long Wan near Sai Kung

197

KENNETH WILLIAMS
ENTERTAINER

*T*he most important milestone in every entertainer's career is his first success. Hong Kong was the place where Kenneth Williams, star of British stage, screen and radio, achieved his first triumph.

Like many comedians of his generation—such as the 'Goons' Peter Sellers, Spike Milligan and Sir Harry Secombe—Williams first trod the boards while a humble squaddy in the British Army.

He was a member of a unit called the CSE (Combined Services Entertainment), which sent him to Hong Kong to perform in a review called *At Your Service* at the China Fleet Club in September 1947. The sailors loved the show.

It was also broadcast on Radio Hong Kong. The success of the review led to Williams appearing in a drama called *The Death of Nelson*, which was aired on ZBW, the forces' broadcast network. The narrator of the programme was an admiral of the fleet.

The Admiral was so pleased with the performance that he invited the complete cast to a cocktail party aboard his flagship. They were driven from the studio in the Admiral's car to HMS *Tamar*, where a guard of honour presented arms as they boarded a launch. With great pomp and ceremony they were were piped aboard the Admiral's flagship.

The cast were in civilian clothes and all went well until it was discovered, during the course of idle conversation, that they were common soldiers. No member of the cast was an officer.

The star of the film *Carry On up the Khyber* described on the BBC, many years later, what happened next: 'Within minutes we were relieved of our drinks, ushered out of the ward room, bundled over the side and sent back to the shore. This time there was no admiral's pennant flying, and we were dispatched without ceremony. Our glory had been short lived.'

HAILE SELASSIE
EMPEROR OF ETHIOPIA

Hong Kong has always had its fair share of royal visitors. It still does. Her Majesty Queen Elizabeth II has made two official visits. Prince Charles has often dropped in and Prince Philip—as President of the World Wide Fund for Nature—has spent a considerable amount of time in the Mai Po marshes, protecting our endangered species. Minor royalty from numerous countries pass through all the time, almost unnoticed, but when an emperor comes to stay—even on a private visit—it is a very rare event.

His Imperial Majesty Haile Selassie, the Lion of Judah and Emperor of Ethiopia, was a direct descendant from King Solomon and the Queen of Sheba. In the early 1950s, he was probably the first reigning emperor to visit Hong Kong since the last Sung emperor, Wei Wong, who took refuge from the Mongol hordes of Kublai Khan in 1277.

The Lion of Judah

When an emperor graces your hotel with his imperial presence, his every whim is your command. Leo Gaddi, the manager of The Peninsula, was anxious to please. Distinguished guests sometimes make strange requests and it was difficult to surprise an old hand like Leo Gaddi, but an imperial command to

replace the Western-style lavatories, was something entirely new.

With ruthless efficiency the hotel's contractors ripped out the British flush toilets and replaced them with the eastern variety, just in time for the royal visit. As the Emperor had taken the whole of the sixth floor west, the logistics were horrendous. Even so, 'Operation Prester John', named after the legendary King of Abyssinia, took only two days. It is reported that the Lion of Judah had a comfortable stay.

Poor Haile Selassie lost his throne in 1974 and died the next year. Like the birds of Mai Po, emperors have become an endangered species. There is now only one left.

His Imperial Majesty, King of Kings, Lord of Lords, Haile Selassie,
Emperor of Ethiopia, with the Governor of Hong Kong, Sir Alexander Grantham

MICHAEL PATRICK O'BRIEN
THE HUMAN YO-YO

When Michael Patrick O'Brien was accused of being a spy by the Shanghai police in 1952, he promptly fled to Macau. He had no papers and was ordered to leave the enclave. As he hadn't any money, he stowed away on a ferry to Hong Kong called the *Lee Hong*.

The British authorities refused to let him land in Hong Kong and the Portuguese would not let him return to Macau. O'Brien spent the next ten dreary months on the ferry, chugging back and forth between the two ports. He became known as the 'Human Yo-Yo'.

At one stage in Shanghai he had worked as a bodyguard for K V Starr, the insurance taipan. Starr paid for his food and the ferry passengers bought him drinks. Occasionally he got drunk and had to be locked up in the ship's brig by the long suffering Captain Rowe. When the *Lee Hong* went into dry dock, so did O'Brien.

Eventually, he was given a visa for Brazil; but when he arrived in Rio de Janeiro they would not let him in. He was soon to be found yo-yoing again between Italy and France. Finally, he ended up in the Dominican Republic, where it is said he became Minister of Culture. The Curt Jurgens and Orson Welles film *The Ferry to Hong Kong* is based on his story.

Throughout this saga, patriotic Irishmen were demanding a fair deal for this unfortunate son of Erin. They got very upset when they discovered that O'Brien was not Irish at all. His real name was Steven Ragan and he was born in Budapest. When he was two years old his family emigrated to America. O'Brien had never taken out American citizenship and was deported after serving seven years hard labour for armed robbery in Oregon. He had arrived in Shanghai without papers in 1931.

CLARK GABLE
FILM STAR

It has been claimed that the Hollywood film star, Clark Gable, introduced the 'Screwdriver' to Hong Kong at the bar of The Peninsula hotel. This is a pleasant mixture of vodka and orange juice, but discerning drinkers tend to prefer to take it without the orange. Gable was making a film called *Soldier of Fortune*, which was eventually released in 1955. This roaring, swashbuckling adventure story was set in Hong Kong. It was not his greatest film. However, it was not quite bad enough to be nominated for an Oscar.

Gable used to sit in the lobby of The Peninsula for hours, chatting

The star of 'Gone with the Wind'
catching up with some light reading

with his friend, Jock, who occupied table number 44. John Prosser-Inglis, which was Jock's real name, lived in the hotel and had claimed this particular table as his own. It was known as 'Jock's Office' and, when Jock was out of his office, a half-full glass was left on the table and nobody else was allowed to sit there.

Unfortunately, the 'King of Hollywood' seemed to spend more time holding court in Jock's Office than he did filming. Finally the producer had had enough. He was forced to put Jock's Office out-of-bounds, otherwise the film would never have been finished.

Jock, as his nickname indicates, was Scottish. In spite of this, he was an immensely generous man, endowed with a great sense of humour. He once gave another of his friends, Felix Bieger, the Assistant Manager of The Peninsula, a clock; probably because Bieger was Swiss.

In the twenty-three years Jock lived in The Peninsula, he only left Hong Kong twice. The last time, he was taken ill on a trip to London, where he died suddenly. At the exact hour of his death, 9,644 kilometres away in Hong Kong, the clock which he had given his pal, Felix Bieger, stopped! It never worked again.

The Peninsula hotel lobby

RICHARD MASON
BRITISH WRITER

For better or for worse, Richard Mason totally changed Hong Kong's image from a delightful, sleepy, tropical, colonial backwater with a funny name—nestling half-forgotten on the south China coast—into a brash, harsh, garish, cesspool of vice and depravity, overburdened by appalling poverty. Since the fifties there have been spectacular changes in Hong Kong, but its image has never really recovered. Richard Mason wrote *The World of Suzie Wong*.

Mason arrived in Hong Kong in 1955 with very little money. The cheapest hotel he could find was the old Luk Kwok in Wanchai, which was pulled down years ago—although a new hotel now bears its name.

He took a room on the fourth floor. It cost him about £1 a night. He had no idea what he had let himself in for.

On the ground floor of the hotel was a bar. The first night Mason dropped in for a drink. The bar was full of girls and sailors. He liked it. We know that Mason left the bar at least twice during his stay in Hong Kong. He

spent a month touring the region with film producer David Lean and we know that the Governor of Hong Kong, Sir Alexander Grantham, invited him to lunch at Government House. The arrival of the Governor's car outside the hotel to pick him up caused a minor sensation.

Mason seems to have spent most of his time chatting-up the local girls and swapping old yarns with sailors. Everything he heard he wrote down. His book was published in 1957. The Broadway show and the film followed. Wanchai was suddenly famous. Mason had put Hong Kong on the map. Hundreds of new girlie bars opened and every bar had at least one bargirl who claimed to be Mason's original Suzie Wong. Considering Richard Mason only spent three months in the Colony, most of it propping up a bar, the impact his visit had on Hong Kong is without equal.

An American sailor snaps a rickshaw man in Wanchai, by Yau Leung, 1966

205

*The old Luk Kwok Hotel,
where Mason stayed*

*William Holden and
Nancy Kwan in
Ray Stark's film,
'The World of Suzie Wong'*

KRISHNA MENON
INDIAN STATESMAN

It was an inopportune time for the Indian statesman, Krishna Menon, to be staying at Government House. In April 1955, Chinese Nationalist agents had just blown up an airliner called the *Kashmir Princess,* which was full of Chinese Communist journalists bound for the Bandung Conference. The bomb had been put on board at Kai Tak Airport and the *Kashmir Princess* belonged to Air India.

At first the Governor, Sir Alexander Grantham, was very impressed by Menon. He was in some ways an awkward guest, particularly when it came to food. He was one of those extremely committed vegetarians who would not even eat eggs, but 'seemed to subsist on innumerable cups of tea into which he would pour a great deal of milk and half a dozen lumps of sugar'.

Menon had just returned from an errand of mercy in China. It had not been a success. He had been trying to persuade the Chinese to release some American airmen they were holding prisoner. Menon proceeded to explain to Grantham, in a rather off-hand manner, that he might be able to get the Chinese to change their minds if Grantham could arrest and execute somebody for blowing up the plane.

Grantham told Menon that the suspected bomber, Chow Chu, had escaped and fled to Taiwan and could not be extradited. He added that, while the police might have a few vague suspicions that a couple of other individuals who might have been involved in the conspiracy were still in the territory, they had absolutely no hard evidence to go on.

Krishna Menon

When Menon suggested casually that a bit of the 'third degree' might be applied to the suspects in order to extract a confession, Grantham was horrified. It was unpleasant to discover that a man whose philosophy did not allow him to eat an egg because it would take the life of an unborn chicken, seemed to have little or no qualms when it came to torturing his fellow human beings.

ORSON WELLES
FILM STAR

The story of the 'Human Yo-Yo', Michael Patrick O'Brien, who spent ten months stuck on the ferry between Macau and Hong Kong, had all the ingredients for a rip-roaring adventure film. Curt Jurgens played the hero and Orson Welles the ship's captain. It was called *The Ferry to Hong Kong* and was shot in the Colony.

Some of the cast were staying at the Luk Kwok Hotel and the director, Lewis Gilbert, asked the hotel's resident bandleader, Nick Demuth, to find him a 'genuine Hong Kong nightclub band'. Nick, whose 'genuine Hong Kong nightclub band' was playing upstairs in The Cactus Room, offered their services; but his band was not considered 'authentic' enough by the director, so a group of dummy musicians were put together instead.

The director wanted some 'authentic' nightclub music. Nick had suggested Johann Strauss's 'Tritsch-Tratsch-Polka' and was immediately dispatched to clear the copyright with a lawyer in Central. This proved impossible, because they had to shoot the scene the next day. 'I wrote the music on the tram to North Point', Nick told me.

The next day the director was sick, so Orson Welles took over. The film company had spent thousands of dollars building a fabulous set; which was far more opulent than anything any nightclub in Hong Kong had to offer. The shooting went smoothly until the fight scene.

Orson liked to do everything himself—with *gusto*—particularly when it came to breaking things. Waving a chair in his hand, he approached the terrified 'dummy' drummer, who was sitting in front of a gorgeous stained glass window, pretending to play the drums. 'When I say duck!' commanded Welles, 'Duck!'

'One, two, three...DUCK!' bellowed Welles. The drummer ducked and Welles hurled the chair through the stained glass window, smashing an expensive arc lamp behind it. It took him most of the day to demolish the rest of set. It was the most expensive scene in the film.

'You couldn't hear my music for all the bangs, crashes and wallops!' complained Nick.

Orson Welles

MICHAEL TODD
SHOWMAN

*T*he Governor of Hong Kong, Sir Alexander Grantham, together with his wife, Lady Maurine, prided themselves on their fabulous dinner parties. They had planned a splendid farewell dinner for the British Naval Commander-in-Chief. Lady Grantham was an American and they had asked the film star Elizabeth Taylor and her husband, Michael Todd, who were visiting Hong Kong, to join the party. It is easy to imagine their delight when they were able to add a touch of royalty to the occasion by inviting, at the last moment, the Crown Prince of Iraq, who had just arrived in Hong Kong unexpectedly. His Highness graciously accepted.

Unfortunately, they knew nothing about the Crown Prince. To Grantham's horror he discovered that the Prince had an anti-Semitic streak in his character and that he had created an unpleasant scene at a party the previous night, because one of the guests happened to be Jewish. Suddenly, the glittering social event seemed to be doomed for absolute disaster because Michael Todd was also Jewish.

Fortunately, Grantham was a skilled and devious diplomat. He explained the situation to Todd and suggested that it might be rather amusing if Todd pretended to be Scottish for the evening. This deception appealed to Todd's sense of humour. He took to the part with unexpected relish. 'The party went off very well', wrote Grantham. 'The handsome Prince, in a dazzling array of decorations, could not have been more charming and agreeable. Elizabeth Taylor was breathtakingly beautiful and Todd was at his most vivacious.'

Even though the dinner was a wild success, Sir Alexander and Lady Grantham breathed a deep sigh of relief when it was over. Whether the Crown Prince ever found out about the deception will never be known. He was murdered a few months after the event.

LORD THOMSON OF FLEET

PRESS BARON

Lord Thomson of Fleet, the Canadian publisher, is perhaps best known for his remark that owning a commercial television company was 'just like having a licence to print your own money'. Apart from his television interests in Britain, he also owned the *Sunday Times* newspaper.

On a visit to Hong Kong in the early 1960s, he went drinking with Richard Hughes, the Far East correspondent of that paper. Hughes, for many years the doyen of Hong Kong's press corps, was a larger-than-life personality who sported a monocle. He was the inspiration behind several characters in books. He is 'Old Craw' in John Le Carré's *The Honourable Schoolboy* and also appears as Dikko Henderson in Ian Fleming's *You Only Live Twice*.

In his book *Hong Kong: Borrowed Place—Borrowed Time*, Hughes tells how he and Lord Thomson went to the famous Wanchai bar in the old Luk Kwok Hotel, where the legend of Suzie Wong was born.

The bar was almost empty apart from a few despondent young girls knitting. There was an enormous golden juke box 'which bellowed and shook'. The two corpulent old men pretended to be a couple of pay-master sergeants of a US aircraft carrier in Victoria Harbour. It is unlikely they really fooled the bargirls who sat down to drink with them. American pay-master sergeants tend not to wear monocles.

As the visit was conducted 'purely in a mood of curiosity and investigation', Hughes was rather surprised when the portly press baron asked his beautiful companion how much it was to go upstairs. The bargirl 'lovingly' told him. He scrawled down the price on the back of the envelope. Her hopes were dashed when he then asked her how much a room cost 'unaccompanied'.

Thomson proceeded to check the price of everything. After the two 'pay-master sergeants' left the hotel, Hughes asked Thomson if he was thinking of buying the place. 'No, but I think I could do worse, don't you think?'

THE BEATLES
POPULAR ENTERTAINERS

$\mathcal{W}$ith bated breath, on a hot June morning in 1964, over a thousand hysterical fans waited for The Beatles to arrive at Kai Tak Airport. Unfortunately, when the 'Fab Four' did arrive there were only three of them—Ringo was conspicuously absent. Wisely they had brought along a substitute Beatle called Jimmy Nichol. Ringo, it seems, was ill.

Their show was a great success, provided that you didn't try to listen seriously to the music. The *South China Morning Post* 'Guest Critic' wrote: 'Their concert at the Princess Theatre last night was a pulsating pandemonium of rhythm and sound which at times made it virtually impossible for a true listener in the audience to hear a thing.' His advice was: 'Don't bother to go. Buy their records and listen to them in the comfort of your living-rooms.'

As there was only one concert—and it was over—this was a pretty useless piece of advice. No wonder he used the pseudonym 'a Guest Critic'. I don't expect that Miss Sophia Sunday, President of the Royal and Faithful Beatle Empire, or Miss Caral Carlotta, President of the Crazy Four Beatle Fan Club International Headquarters, who were at the concert, were worried too much about not being able to hear the music.

Substitute drummer, Jimmy Nichol, was the only Beatle who bothered to go sight-seeing. 'He is so humble,' explained his escort, fifteen-year-old Filipina singing star, Baby Aguilar.

Two years later, the love affair between the Beatles and the Filipinos came to an abrupt end when they failed to turn up to a lunch, given in their honour by First Lady Imelda Marcos at the Presidential Palace in Manila.

When questioned by reporters, John Lennon answered enigmatically, 'Woof! Woof!' The Liverpudlians left Manila airport amidst shouts of 'Beatles go home!' from a hostile crowd. When asked about their reception in Manila, pacifist George Harrison said: 'If I go back it will be with an H-Bomb to drop on it.'

The Beatles in Hong Kong, without Ringo Starr

PIERRE TRUDEAU
PRIME MINISTER OF CANADA

The Prime Minister of Canada, Pierre Trudeau, dropped into Hong Kong for a weekend on his way to Expo '70 in Osaka. On the Saturday night he was to be guest of honour at a Chinese dinner party at the Mandarin Hotel, given by the Canadian Trade Commissioner, Mr C R Gallow.

On the following Sunday morning he attended mass at the Cathedral of the Immaculate Conception in Caine Road. Later on he visited Sai Wan War Cemetery, where he laid a wreath and paid his respects to the gallant officers and men of the Winnipeg Grenadiers and Royal Rifles of Canada, who gave their lives during the defence of Hong Kong in 1941.

He had lunch on a floating restaurant in Aberdeen and spent the afternoon on the

Pierre Trudeau

beach. He later made a courtesy call on the Governor, Sir David Trench.

Having paid his respects to Chinese cuisine, the Canadian community, Governor Trench, God and the Glorious Dead, 'the world's most eligible bachelor' hit the town, dressed casually in white slacks and a navy blue T-shirt.

His choice of garments failed to impress the doorman of the Scene Discotheque, who refused to let him in because he was not wearing a jacket. Undeterred he went on to a bar. At that time there were seven

214

bars in the colony with 'Playboy' in their name and two with 'Playgirl'.
None of the them had anything whatsoever to do with Hugh Hefner.
Trudeau chose the Universal Playboy, which was housed below the
offices of the Lutheran Church, at 69 Peking Road, Kowloon.

It was reported in the *Hongkong Standard* that Trudeau's Chinese
'date (as yet unnamed)—a diminutive five foot three girl in a red, cotton
flowered dress—was possibly a little overawed by the whole thing. She
seemed to be very shy and when they were on the floor she seemed to
be waiting for Mr Trudeau to make the first move'.

Floating restaurants at Aberdeen

POPE PAUL VI
PONTIFF

'*P*ope Paul prayed for peace today amid the most fantastic security precautions ever taken in Hongkong,' reported the *China Mail* on 4 December 1970. 'Detectives with binoculars and walkie talkies dotted the rooftops in Happy Valley as the Pope blessed thousands of school children at the racecourse.'

A few days earlier, Pope Paul VI had been attacked by a mad and crazed Bolivian artist, Benjamin Mendoza Y Arnor, at Manila airport: 'President Marcos, a war-time guerrilla leader, parried the dagger thrust, pushed the Pope away and gave Mendoza a karate chop.'

However, in Hong Kong, there was no valiant Marcos on hand to fend off potential assassins; only the Acting Governor, Sir Hugh Norman-Walker, assisted by a few thousand stalwarts of the Royal Hong Kong Police.

Because of the religious significance of the occasion, it was deemed appropriate that the guardians of the law should wear plainclothes. This created a problem: how does one plainclothes policeman recognize another plainclothes policeman?

The answer can be found in the photographs of the Pontiff's visit. Wherever he went, his Holiness was surrounded by a mob of large men with short hair, big shoulders and unsightly bulges under their arm-pits—and sometimes elsewhere. Apart from wearing similar ill-fitting suits, they sported absolutely identical ties.

By a fortunate coincidence, the Royal Hong Kong Police Force's tie has purple and gold stripes, which are the Vatican colours; not that any assassin would necessarily appreciate this sartorial phenomenon.

The Pope later celebrated mass at the Government Stadium. There was disappointment that he only spent three hours in Hong Kong 'the largest Chinese diocese in this world', as opposed to sixteen hours in the 'world's largest Moslem country, Indonesia'.

In spite of all the security precautions, the Pope did not leave Hong Kong entirely unscathed. Twelve days after his visit, the *China Mail* ran the headline: 'Pope Paul down with Hongkong flu'.

*Pope Paul VI with the Acting Governor,
Sir Hugh Norman-Walker*

The old Catholic Cathedral

FRANCIS JAMES
AUSTRALIAN JOURNALIST

During troubled times journalists can sometimes be rocketed to fame by being taken prisoner, held hostage or arrested for espionage. The imprisonment of Anthony Grey, Reuter's correspondent in Peking during the Cultural Revolution, turned him into a household name.

While the British public were justifiably enraged over the outrageous incarceration of Grey, another British journalist, sixty-nine-year-old Norman Barrymaine, managed (with some difficulty) to get himself arrested for spying in Shanghai. Barrymaine was then subsequently interrogated continuously for nineteen months by the Chinese.

The object of an interrogator is to get the prisoner to talk. In Barrymaine's case it was impossible to stop him. He allegedly broke the spirit of his interrogators by boring them to tears.

When the news broke that Francis James, the editor of an obscure Australian newspaper called the *Anglican*, was to be released by the Chinese, there was a certain amount of cynicism in Hong Kong. It was generally suspected that James, a flamboyant figure with an eccentric taste in headgear, had deliberately got himself arrested in his quest for fame.

His entrance into Hong Kong could not have been more dramatic. As he crossed the border, he collapsed into the arms of John Slimming, the Director of the Hong Kong Government Information Services. James was wearing a silly hat at the time.

He was whisked away to the Matilda Hospital, where he was photographed sitting up in bed with another silly hat perched on his pate. James had sold his story to *The Age* and the *Sydney Morning Herald*, but he seemed to be in no hurry to commit his experiences to paper.

The sterile hygienic atmosphere of an hospital ward was obviously not conducive to the release of his creative juices. In Australia he used an old 1936 Rolls Royce as an office and could often be seen typing away in the back seat while parked in the middle of Sydney.

While he was possibly too exhausted to write, he was not too exhausted to talk—and talk he did! He foolishly gave an interview to Greg Clark of a rival newspaper, the *Australian*. The garrulous James told all. Clark printed everything he said and scooped him with his own story.

RMS QUEEN ELIZABETH
MONARCH OF THE SEAS

"QUEEN ELIZABE[

*A*nyone who has ever witnessed a great ship in its death throes can only be convinced that she was once a living being. It is an awesome sight. The great Cunard liner *RMS Queen Elizabeth* caught fire and sunk in the western harbour aproaches of Hong Kong in 1972.

Painted battleship grey, the liner made her maiden voyage during World War Two, when she and her sister ship, the *Queen Mary*, were used as troop ships. 'Built for the arts of peace and to link the Old World to the New,' wrote Winston Churchill. 'The Queens challenged the fury of Hitlerism in the Battle of the Atlantic.'

After the war she reverted to her original function of a luxury liner. By 1967 she was losing US$1.8 million a year and was due to be scrapped. The ship lovers of the world were delighted when C Y Tung, a Hong Kong shipping magnate, bought the *Queen Elizabeth* for US$3 million and so saved her from becoming a maritime fun-fair.

C Y Tung completely refitted the grand old lady as a floating learning institute and renamed her 'Seawise University' (i.e. C Y's University). On 9 January 1972, just five days before the renovation work was expected to be completed, several mysterious fires broke out on board. It was a Sunday and the Hong Kong Journalists' Association was having a barbecue at Chi Ma Wan Prison, hosted by a character known as 'Dick the Drop', a former hangman. Stranded on Lantau Island, many reporters missed their deadlines.

The court of enquiry's findings were not very helpful: 'The Court regrets that it is unable to assign a certain cause to any of the fires but considers...that the most probable cause in each case was acts of a person or persons unknown.'

The burnt-out hulk became a tourist attraction. It was even used as Q's headquarters in the James Bond film *The Man with the Golden Gun*. It was a dismal end for a monarch of the seas.

220

A poster of RMS Queen Elizabeth, autographed
by the captain and crew of the liner's last voyage

The 'Monarch of the Seas' in flames

The burnt out hulk of RMS Queen Elizabeth in the western harbour approaches

223

CHARLES SOBHRAJ
MASS MURDERER

*I*t is unlikely that Charles Sobhraj and his unsavoury creatures, Marie Andrée Leclerc and Ajay Chowdury, murdered anyone in Hong Kong. Sobhraj had a healthy respect for the Royal Hong Kong Police. However, the double murder which eventually put the law on his trail had its origins in Hong Kong. Sobhraj preyed mainly on backpackers.

The 1970s were golden years for hippies. Thousands of 'flower children' boarded ramshackle buses and old vans in Europe and trekked overland to Nepal and India—via Afghanistan—before spreading like a virus all over Southeast Asia.

Many of these wanderers came from middle-class families and, despite an outward appearance of poverty, often carried large sums of money. In many Asian countries they were regarded as pests and, if they were robbed, the police were unlikely to take action. Many of them went missing only to reappear, months later, in another Asian country. They were ideal victims.

Cornelia Hemker and Henricus Bintanja, a Dutch couple, were staying at the International Guest House in Chungking Mansions, Kowloon, when they ran into Sobhraj. Posing as a gem dealer, he sold Hemker a sapphire ring at a bargain price. Anyone who could afford to buy gems must have money.

Sobhraj's basic *modus operandi* was simple. He would put a laxative in his victims' drinks. When they were struck down with diarrhoea, he would provide them with phoney medication in the form of a knock out pill. When they eventually woke up they had lost their money, their passports and the gems which he had sold them; and Sobhraj had vanished.

He lured the Dutch couple to Thailand, where he robbed and murdered them. His next door neighbours were suspicious. They reported his activities to the Dutch Consul. Sobhraj and his gang, after being questioned by the Thai police, fled the country.

Seven months later, he doped a group of French students at the Vikram Hotel in Delhi. Something went wrong and soon twenty odd students were falling down and vomiting all over the lobby. He and Leclerc were arrested by the Indian Police on 5 July 1976. Leclerc died in custody, but Sobhraj escaped from gaol a few years later. He was later recaptured and still languishes in gaol in India.

Chungking Mansions, Nathan Road

Charles Sobhraj in the custody of the Indian Police in New Delhi

IMELDA MARCOS
FIRST LADY OF THE PHILIPPINES

*H*ong Kong's aviation buffs and environmentalists were in a tizzy. The Anglo-French supersonic airliner Concorde was coming. The plane touched down at 3.51 pm at Kai Tak Airport on 6 November 1976—one day ahead of schedule. It was not its supersonic speed that accounted for Concorde's early arrival, but Imelda Marcos, the wife of the President of the Philippines.

The aircraft was on a sales promotion tour of the Far East when the First Lady hijacked it for a side trip to Hong Kong. She only stayed for three hours. The newspapers suggested, rather unkindly, that Mrs Marcos had come to Hong Kong on a 'shopping spree'. This dastardly allegation was absolutely untrue! Mrs Marcos had come to Hong Kong for lunch. Her party was driven directly from Kai Tak to The Peninsula, where a magnificent banquet awaited them in the Marco Polo Suite.

While Imelda and her cronies were gorging themselves on champagne and caviar, the sixteen members of Concorde's international air crew were stuck at Kai Tak. The swiftness with which the First Lady had

Mrs Imelda Marcos and her party heading for lunch at The Peninsula hotel

The Anglo-French supersonic airliner, Concorde, at Kai Tak airport

commandeered Concorde had taken the crew quite by surprise. They
had left their passports behind in Manila and Hong Kong's immigration
officials had refused to allow them to leave the airport.

At 7.18 pm, Concorde, with a very well-fed First Lady aboard, flew
back to Manila. It returned to Hong Kong the next day on its
official visit.

In spite of the heroic efforts of the French *Aerospatiale Compagnie*
and the British Aircraft Corporation's sales team, Philippine Airlines
did not buy a single Concorde aircraft. The environmentalists were also
disappointed. Their gloomy predictions that the noise level would prove
a health hazard to anyone living on the shores of Kai Tak Nullah turned
out to be completely unfounded. Concorde proved to be only slightly
noisier than the Boeing 707.

MOTHER TERESA
ITINERANT NUN

*P*eople generally visit Hong Kong to go shopping, eat delicious Chinese food or to enjoy the delightful sights and smells of the 'East'. There was one visitor who, on arriving in Hong Kong in 1985, headed straight for an establishment called, interestingly, the 'Home of Love'.

At that time, the Home of Love was a 480-square-metre, single-storey structure known as 'Hut 291' and was bang right in the middle of what was once Shamshuipo Army Camp. The building was leased from the Lands Department for one Hong Kong dollar a year. This must have been the lowest rent of any building in the colony at the time. The visitor, who was also the new tenant, described the hut as 'a beautiful place'.

Two years later, the visitor returned to Hong Kong and again went straight to the Home of Love. One of the women occupants, Miss Lee Woon Ho, told the visitor: 'I feel comfortable living here. At least I don't have cockroaches and rats running around on my bed.'

Miss Lee was one of the twenty-two destitute women living in the Home of Love. She claimed to be 107 years old. The visitor was a Roman Catholic nun called Mother Teresa, who won the Nobel Peace Prize in 1979 for her work among the poor in the slums of Calcutta.

Mother Teresa founded the 'Missionaries of Charity' to take care of the needy. Almost everywhere in the world where there was poverty, the nuns of the order were there. When Mother Teresa indicated that she wanted to help the poor in China, the Chinese government's response was that, as they were revolutionaries, they did not require her help. This invoked a spirited reply: 'My work too is revolutionary, not ordinary social service. The people who have nothing, who have nobody, who have forgotten what human joy is, who are rejected, unwanted, unloved, uncared, hungry, naked or homeless—these are our people.'

China's loss was Hong Kong's gain: Mother Teresa had opened her Home of Love in Shamshuipo.

Mother Teresa

MADONNA
SEX SYMBOL

'Target Madonna!' screamed the *Hongkong Standard* in January 1986—and the hunt was on! With bulldog tenacity, Hong Kong's intrepid press corps rushed hotfoot in pursuit of the Material Girl and her violent husband, whom they branded as Sean 'Poison' Penn.

However, one newshound did not join the hunt. The ear of Ian Markham-Smith, the editor of the *Hong Kong Tatler*, had come into sharp contact with a brick wielded by Penn a year earlier in the parking lot of the Maxwell House Hotel in Nashville, Tennessee. Markham-Smith reckoned that to be hit by Sean Penn once was unfortunate, but to be hit by him twice would be sheer carelessness.

Hong Kong's newshounds cornered their prey in the Oriental Hotel in Macau where, to their delight, Penn 'allegedly' grabbed at a camera, bruising the neck of sixty-one-year-old paparazzo Leonel Borralhio, who was a former member of Macau's *Leal Senado* (Loyal Senate). This was the stuff that news is made of! But still, alas, no interviews.

From the window of a room on the seventh floor of the Oriental Hotel, *South China Morning Post* reporter, Nicola Parkinson, spotted Madonna having a tennis lesson. The intrepid Nicola rushed down to the third floor, hoping to catch the star in the lift. She bumped into Madonna's bodyguard outside the health centre. 'I popped my head around the corner of the changing room,' wrote Nicola, 'and saw Madonna getting undressed.'

Five minutes later Nicola was in the sauna. 'Madonna was sitting on the upper shelf, wrapped in an orange towel, in the lotus position.' Nicola's interview was going smoothly until a Madonna video appeared on the television screen in the sauna. 'This seemed to annoy her. She put down her magazine, drew her knees up to her chin, sighed deeply and rested her forehead on her arms as though trying to block the noise out.'

There were two Chinese girls in the sauna. Their eyes were glued to the screen, blissfully unaware that the steamy sex goddess, whose image they were watching, was sitting right behind them.

Madonna Cicconne

BIBLIOGRAPHY

Auden, W.H. and Christopher Isherwood, *Journey to a War*, Faber & Faber Ltd, London, 1939.

Augustin, Andreas, *The Peninsula*, Andreas Augustin, 1988.

Baillie, Rev. John, *A Memoir of Captain W. Thornton Bate, RN*, Longman, Brown, Green, Longmans & Roberts, London, 1859.

Balfour, S.F., *Hong Kong before the British*, The Journal of the Hong Kong Branch of the Royal Asiatic Society, 1940.

Bard, Solomon, *Traders of Hong Kong: Some Foreign Merchant Houses, 1841-1899*, Urban Council, Hong Kong, 1993.

Barrett, Ken, *He Knew Suzie*, Hong Kong Tatler Annual, 1989.

Beach, Rev. William, *Visit of HRH The Duke of Edinburgh to Hong Kong*, Smith Elder & Co., London, 1870.

Birch, Alan, *Hong Kong: The Colony That Never Was*, Odyssey, Hong Kong, 1991

Bird, Isabella, *The Golden Cheronese: Travels in Malaya in 1879*, Oxford University Press, Kuala Lumpur, 1967.

Bird, Isabella, *Unbeaten Tracks in Japan*, George Newnes, 1990.

Blakeney, William, *The Coasts of Cathay and Cipango Forty Years Ago*, Elliot Stock, London, 1902.

Burkhardt, V.R., *Chinese Creeds and Customs*, South China Morning Post, 1955.

Catchpole, Brian, *A Map History of Modern China*, Heinemann, London, 1976.

Champley, Henry, *The Road to Shanghai*, John Long Ltd, London, 1934.

Chao, G.H., *The Life and Times of Sir Kai Ho Kai*, The Chinese University Press, Hong Kong, 1981.

Churchill, Allen, *The Roosevelts*, Harper and Row.

Coates, Austin, *China Races*, Oxford University Press, Hong Kong, 1983.

Coates, P.D., *The China Consuls*, Oxford University Press, Hong Kong, 1988.

Cooke, George Wingrove, *The Times*, London.

Coward, Sir Noel, *The Lyrics of Noel Coward*, Methuen, London, 1983.

Cree, Edward, *The Cree Journals*, Webb & Bower, Exeter, 1981.

Deakin, F.W. and Storey G.R., *The Case of Richard Sorge*, Chatto & Windus, London, 1966.

Deakin, Richard, *The Chinese Secret Service*, Ballantine Books, New York, 1974.

De Leeuw, Hendrik, *Cities of Sin*, Noel Douglas Ltd, London, 1934.

Dougherty, Paul, *Hong Kong 1968*, *Hong Kong 1969* and *Hong Kong 1970*, Hong Kong Government Information Services.

Drage, Charles, *General of Fortune*, Heineman, London, 1963.

Drage, Charles, *Two-Gun Cohen*, Jonathan Cape, London, 1954.

Dyer Ball, J., *Things Chinese*, John Murray, London, 1904.

Eitel, E.J., *Europe in China: The History of Kong Kong*, Kelly & Walsh, Hong Kong, 1895.

Endacott, G.B., *A Biographical Sketch-book of Early Hong Kong*, Eastern Universities Press, Singapore, 1962.

Endacott, G.B., *A History of Hong Kong*, Oxford University Press, London, 1958.

Fox, Grace, *British Admirals and Chinese Pirates 1832-1869*, Kegan Paul, Trench, Trubner & Co., London, 1940.

Grantham, Sir Alexander, *Via Ports*, Hong Kong University Press, 1965.

Guinness, Geraldine, *In the Far East*, Morgan & Scott, 1889.

Hacker, Arthur and Perkins David, *Hacker's Hong Kong*, Gareth Powell & Ted Thomas, Hong Kong, 1976.

Hake, Egmont, *The Story of Chinese Gordon*, Remington & Co., London, 1884.

Hall, Capt Basil, *Voyage to the Eastern Seas*, Archibald Constable & Co., London. 1826.

Harfield, Alan, *British and Indian Armies on the China Coast 1785-1985*, A & J Partnership, 1990.

Hoe, Susanna, *The Private Life of Old Hong Kong*, Oxford University Press, Hong Kong, 1991.

Hogbottle, Sebastian & ffuckes, Simon, *Snatches & Lays*, Boozy Company, Melbourne, 1962.

Hopkirk, Peter, *The Great Game*, John Murray, 1990.

Hughes, Richard, *Hong Kong: Borrowed Place—Borrowed Time*, Andre Deutsh, London, 1968.

Hurd, Douglas, *The Arrow War*, Collins, London, 1967.

Hutcheon, Robin, *Souvenirs of Borget*, South China Morning Post, 1979.

Jasen, David A., *P.G. Wodehouse: A Portrait of a Master*, Continuum, New York, 1974.

Johnston, Reginald, *Twilight in the Forbidden City*, Victor Gollancz Ltd, London, 1934.

Jung Chang, *Mme Sun Yat-Sen*, Penguin Books, London, 1986.

Kipling, Rudyard, *From Sea to Sea*, MacMillan & Co. Ltd, 1900.

Kipling, Rudyard, *The White Man's Burden*, 1899, *Rudyard Kipling's Verse*, Hodder & Stoughton, 1912.

Lai, T.C., *The Eight Immortals*, Swindon Book Company, Hong Kong, 1972.

Lampson, Miles, *Diary*, 1906.

Larkin, Philip, *Collected Poems*, The Marvell Press and Faber & Faber, London, 1988.

Lee, James Zee-Ming, *Chinese Potpourri*, Oriental Publishers, Hong Kong, 1950.

Lethbridge, Henry, *Hong Kong: Stability and Change*, Oxford University Press, Hong Kong, 1978.

Luff, John, *Hong Kong Cavalcade*, South China Morning Post, 1968.

McAleavy, Henry, *The Modern History of China*, Weidenfeld & Nicholson, London, 1967.

Maddocks, Melvin, *The Great Liners*, Time-Life Books, NY, 1982.

Mao Tse-tung, *Basic Tactics*, Frederick A. Praeger, New York, 1966.

McLeod, John, *The Voyage of HMS Alceste*, John Murray, 1819.

Mason, Richard, *The World of Suzie Wong*, William Collins & Co., 1957.

Mattock, Kate, *The Story Of Government House*, Hong Kong Government Information Services, 1978.

Michener, James A., *Rascals in Paradise*, Martin Secker & Warburg, 1957.

Neville, Richard and Clark, Julie, *The Life and Crimes of Charles Sobhraj*, Jonathan Cape, London, 1979.

Norton-Kyshe, James, *The History of the Laws and Courts of Hong Kong*, Vetch & Lee, Hong Kong, 1971.

Oliphant, Laurence, *Narrative of the Earl of Elgin's Mission to China and Japan*, William Blackwood, 1859.

Phillips, Sir Percival, *The Prince of Wales' Eastern Book*, Hodder & Stoughton, London, 1922.

Pope-Hennessy, James, *Verandah*, George Allen & Unwin, London, 1964.

Ram, Vernon, *The Correspondent*, Hong Kong, October 1991.

Roads, David, *Notes on General Emilio Aguinaldo y Fame*.

Roads, David, *Notes on Dr Rizal*.

Robinson, Keith, *Hong Kong 1967*, Hong Kong Government Information Services, 1968.

Rodwell, Sally, *Historic Hong Kong*, Odyssey, Hong Kong, 1991.

Sayer, G.R., *Hong Kong 1862-1919*, Hong Kong University Press, 1975.

Seagrave, Sterling, *The Soong Dynasty*, Sidgwick & Jackson Ltd, London, 1985.

Sergeant, Harriet, *Shanghai*, Jonathan Cape, London, 1991.

Sinclair, Keith, *A Soldier's View of Empire: Reminiscences of James Bodell*, London, 1982.

Smith, Albert, *To China and Back*, Hong Kong University Press, 1974.

Spackman, Jack, *The Correspondent*, Hong Kong, October 1992.

Thomas, David, *Royal Admirals*, Andre Deutsh, London, 1982.

Tuchman, Barbara, *Stilwell and the American Experience in China 1911-1945*, Macmillan, London, 1971.

Turner, John, *Kwang Tung or Five Years in China*, S.W. Partridge & Co., 1894.

Warner, John, *Hong Kong Illustrated: Views and News 1840-1890*, John Warner Publications, Hong Kong, 1981.

Wasserstein, Bernard, *The Secret Lives of Trebitsch Lincoln*, Penguin Books, London, 1989.

Wiethoff, Bodo, *Introduction to Chinese History*, Thames & Hudson, 1971.

White, Walter, *China Station 1859-1864*, National Maritime Museum, Greenwich, 1972.

Wolff, Leon, *Little Brown Brother*, Oxford University Press, Hong Kong, 1991.

Worswick, Clark, *Japan in Photographs 1854-1905*, Hamish Hamilton, London, 1980.

Wortham, H.E., *Chinese Gordon*, Little, Brown and Co., Boston, 1933.

PERIODICALS CONSULTED

The China Mail
The Correspondent
The Friend of China
The Hongkong Daily Press
The Hongkong Register
The Hongkong Standard
The Hong Kong Tatler
The Hongkong Telegraph
The Hongkong Weekly Press
The Illustrated London News
The Journal of the Hong Kong Branch of the Royal Asiatic Society
The South China Morning Post
The Times

TAPES

The British Broadcasting Corporation

INDEX